50 Christmas Crafts

STEP-BY-STEP

50 Christmas Crafts

Penny Boylan

Photographs by Janine Hosegood

SMITHMARK

This edition published in 1996 by
Smithmark Publishers, a division of U.S. Media Holdings, Inc., 16 East 32nd Street,
New York, NY 10016.

SMITHMARK books are available for bulk purchase for sales promotion and for
premium use. For details write or call the manager of special sales, SMITHMARK
Publishers. 16 East 32nd Street, New York, 10016; (212) 532-6600

Produced by Anness Publishing Limited
1 Boundary Row
London SE1 8HP

Printed and bound in Hong Kong

10 9 8 7 6 5 4 3 2 1

CONTENTS

INTRODUCTION

There's no time like Christmas. Sooner or later we all get swept up in its huge, warm embrace. It may be commercialized, expensive and a lot of hard work, but it can also be a magical time of happy gatherings and memorable meals, reaffirming friendships and family ties.

It's an unrivalled opportunity to give free rein to your creativity as you decorate your home and plan your Christmas table. Lighten the dark days of winter with the glint of gold, the enchanting glow of candlelight and the scent of freshly gathered evergreens. The fifty craft ideas in this book will spark your creative energy and help you make the best of the festive season.

You'll find suggestions for traditional, colourful tree ornaments, or you might prefer the elegant monochromic arrangements of gold or silver. If you'd rather get right away from Christmas glitz, find inspiration in a rustic scheme, using materials such as homespun fabrics, natural (garden) raffia, and twigs and greenery you could collect on a winter walk.

Don't stop at decorations: make your own gift-wrap and tags – and gifts too. Find out how to make your own crackers and you'll be able to fill them with personalized treats for your guests.

All the projects are simple to make following the detailed step-by-step instructions. Perhaps they'll introduce you to some new skills, such as needlepoint or stencilling, that you'll want to develop after the flurry of Christmas is over.

Once you've discovered the satisfaction that comes from creating your own Christmas you'll no longer be content with ready-made decorations. Assemble a collection of rich fabrics, gold paper, ribbons, glitter and paint and use them to turn your home into a welcoming haven every Christmastide.

Papers, Paints and Decorating Materials

Build up a store of interesting materials for your decorating projects: save pretty boxes, foil wrappings and packaging material. Specialist crafts suppliers offer a huge range of paints and papers. Remember that gold papers, markers and paints tend to be in short supply near Christmas so it's best to stock up beforehand. Below are some key materials for Christmas crafts.

crepe paper

copper foil

aluminium foil

Crayons and Pens
Stencil crayons come in a range of plain and metallic colours. They are oil-based and dry out to form a skin which must be scraped away each time they are used. Allow the work to dry thoroughly for a permanent finish. Gold (magic) marker pens are an alternative to paint when you need a fine line.

Decorative Papers
The choice is endless here. Look for double-sided and metallic crepe paper, especially in unusual colours such as bronze. Gold papers and foils come in various textures, matt and shiny, and add a touch of luxury to your work. Don't forget the basics: add your own decorations to brown parcel wrap (packaging paper), white paper and card (cardboard).

Glitter and Glitter Paints
There is an amazing selection of different types of glitter to choose from now. As well as the old-fashioned tubes of coloured glitter to sprinkle on, you can buy coloured glitter suspended in clear paint and tubes of glittery fabric paints.

Lino-Cutting Tool
I used this to cut decorative grooves in citrus fruit. A traditional implement, used by chefs, is known as a canelle knife.

Metal Foils
Copper and aluminium foils are available from crafts suppliers in a heavier gauge than ordinary kitchen foil.

Paints
Gold spray paint is useful for covering large areas, but look out for different shades of gold in water-based and oil-based paints. Watercolour inks have a wonderful translucent vibrancy that is quite different to the matt effect of gouache paint. Try to use special stencil paint for stencilling on fabric and paper as it has a creamy texture and will not bleed easily.

Papers
There is a tremendous range of decorative papers available from stationers, crafts suppliers and art shops. It is always worth stocking up at Christmas time as the shops tend to have an even larger selection than usual.

Polystyrene Shapes (Forms)
These are available from crafts suppliers and come in a large range of different shapes.

Oil-based Paints
These paints are used for decorating surfaces that will need washing, such as glass and ceramics. Read the manufacturer's instructions before you use them. Clean brushes with (distilled) turpentine or white spirit (paint thinner). Glass (relief) outliner paint comes in a tube and is squeezed directly on to the surface. It needs a long drying time but sets rock hard.

White Emulsion (Latex) Paint
This is a cheaper alternative to white gouache paint for covering the surface of papier mâché. For added strength, mix in some PVA (white) glue.

Willow Twigs
Perfect for rustic decorations like the little hanging stars on page 53, willow twigs grow straight and regular, and are an excellent material for weaving wreaths. Leave them in their natural state, or paint or spray them.

card
(cardboard)

metallic
crepe paper

gold relief
outliner

stencil crayons

white
paper

WINSOR & NEW
DESIGNE
GOUAC

PERMANEN
WHITE

Blanc-Permanent
Permanentweiß
Blanco Permanente

1.25 US fl.oz
e 37ml

white emulsion
(latex) paint

jaune orangé

Couleurs
vitrail

GOLD/OR
773

Markal
ARTISTS
PAINTSTIK

GUITAR OIL PASTEL
GUITAR OIL PASTEL
GUITAR OIL PASTEL

IRISE

foam board

gouache

oil-based
glass paint

lino-cutting tool

MITCHELL
ENGLAND

decorative
papers

watercolour

gold water
based paint

glitter

poly
shape

gold oil-based
paint

glitter

CONTAIN NO XYLENE

gold (magic)
marker pen

willow twigs

foil wrappers

Fabrics, Ribbons, Trims and Threads

One of the joys of making your own original decorations lies in using high-quality, sumptuous materials: you can create an impression of great luxury with very small amounts of beautiful fabrics, so hunt around for pretty colours and interesting textures as well as unusual ribbons and braids.

Buttons

Many people collect buttons for pleasure. For decorations, keep a supply of gold buttons and always save real mother-of-pearl buttons from shirts that are no longer used. Be on the look out for odd luxury buttons on old jackets which you can use in decorations.

Checked Cotton, Ticking, Wool, Calico, Hessian (Burlap) and Linen

As an antidote to all the richness of traditional Christmas fabrics, simple country-style homespun materials are perfect for naïve decorations. Age fabrics by washing well, then dipping in strong tea. Hessian (burlap) is normally used for upholstery, but its rustic texture and honey colour work very well with bright colours and gold.

Cords and Braids

Gold is the most festive colour for cords and braid, although rich dark colours make an interesting alternative for trimming items you may wish to leave out for the rest of the year. Use fine gold cord to make loops for hanging decorations for the tree.

Polyester Wadding (Batting)

This is invaluable for stuffing since it is lightweight and very soft. It can also be purchased in lengths, for quilting, which can be cut to shape when a light padding is needed.

Ribbons

Wide satin ribbon is the kind most often used for the projects in this book. It is readily available in a versatile range of sizes and colours, sometimes with printed designs. Collect special ribbons when you see them for making tree ornaments and decorating floral displays. Wire-edged ribbon is particularly good for making bows since it holds its shape.

Sequins and Beads

Sequins, seed pearls (heads) and glass beads add instant opulence to any decorative piece. They are available from crafts suppliers in a multitude of shapes and colours. You can also buy plastic "gemstones" to make jewelled ornaments for the tree.

Silks, Taffeta, Organza (Organdy) and Lamé

Use these luxurious fabrics for both decorations and gifts.

You'll find plenty of gold shades to choose from in the run-up to Christmas, but wonderful striped and checked silk can be found all year round.

String and Raffia

I have used thin garden twine for several of the projects in this book: its soft brown colour and rustic appearance suit the naïve decorations. Sisal parcel string and natural (garden) raffia are also used.

Tapestry Canvas

You will need white canvas with 24 holes to 5 cm (12 holes to 1 in) for the needlepoint projects in this book.

Threads

A well-stocked sewing box filled with every shade of sewing thread one could ever need is every dressmaker's dream. Start with essential black and white threads and build up your collection as you sew. Stranded embroidery thread (floss) has six strands: for all but the boldest stitches you'll probably want to use two or three. Cut a length, then pull the strands gently apart. Tapestry wool (yarn) is made for canvas work and is very hard-wearing. Don't be tempted to substitute knitting wool (yarn) or you will be frustrated by constant breaks as you stitch.

Velvet

In rich, dark colours, velvet is especially Christmassy. It is available in light weights for dressmaking and heavier weights for furnishing (upholstering). Look for textured and two-toned velvets.

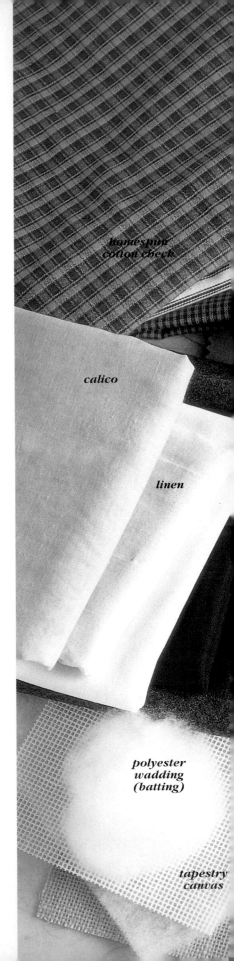

homespun cotton check

calico

linen

polyester wadding (batting)

tapestry canvas

pleated organza

lamé

cotton ticking

gold netting

fine gold cord

decorative braid

sequin ribbon

gold braid

silk

mother-of-pearl buttons

glass beads

plastic gemstones

sequins

satin ribbons

wool

sewing thread

garden twine

stranded embroidery thread (floss)

tapestry wool (yarn)

quilting wadding (batting)

sisal (parcel string)

hessian (burlap)

natural (garden) raffia

Equipment

It's sensible to make sure you have everything you need for your project before you begin. The following list of invaluable equipment includes artists' materials, office supplies and some general bits and pieces you probably already have around the home.

Adhesive Tape
Double-sided adhesive (cellophane) tape allows you to join paper invisibly. It is also a good substitute for glue when you don't wish to dampen a surface, when using crepe paper, for example. Masking tape is indispensable for securing stencils and patterns in position.

Craft Knife
Craft knives have extremely sharp blades. Use them (on a cutting mat) for cutting out stencils and for accurate cutting of paper against a metal ruler. Change the blade frequently and keep out of the reach of children.

Foam Rollers
These come in assorted sizes and are easily washable. Use them with stencil paint and for sponging water-based paints on to paper or fabrics.

Glue
PVA (white) glue is a thick liquid that dries to a transparent sheen. It will stick most surfaces together. It can also be diluted with water when making papier mâché or as a protective coating. After use, wash brushes out in water straight away. Glue-sticks are excellent for sticking paper neatly and are safe for children to use.

Hole Punch
Useful for making neat holes for the handles of gift bags and for punching a single hole in home-made gift tags.

Hot Glue Gun
The best thing to use when you need a glue that dries almost instantly and is very strong and clean. The nozzle delivers a small dot of hot, melted glue at the squeeze of the trigger.

Metal Ruler
This provides a safe edge to work against when cutting paper with a craft knife; you can also use it for measuring and marking out. Use a dressmaker's tape for longer measurements.

Paintbrushes
Old brushes are useful for applying glue and emulsion (latex) paint mixed with PVA (white) glue. Stencil brushes are wide and stiff. You will also need a fine-tipped brush for more delicate work and a medium bristle brush for applying metallic craft paint, which should be cleaned with white spirit (paint thinner) or a commercial brush cleaner.

Pencils and Pens
A soft pencil that can easily be erased is useful for tracing and transferring motifs. Keep an old ballpoint pen that has run out of ink for making embossed foil decorations. For marking light fabrics you can use a vanishing fabric marker: the best fade naturally and don't need to be washed out.

Pins and Needles
Use dressmaker's pins to hold fabrics in place. You'll need an ordinary sewing needle for seams and an embroidery needle with a large eye to thread stranded embroidery thread (floss). A tapestry needle is fairly broad, with a large eye and a blunt point.

Plastic Adhesive
This malleable substance is used for attaching objects and paper to surfaces from which it can later be removed cleanly. It is useful when working with candles to keep them upright in their holders.

Saucers and Jars
Keep old saucers and jars for mixing paint and glue. Keep the lids of the jars, too, so that the contents don't dry out.

Scissors
You will need one pair for cutting paper and another for fabrics: never use the latter on paper as it will blunt them very quickly. A small pair of needlework scissors with pointed ends is useful for embroidery.

Secateurs (Pruning Shears)
For heavy-duty foliage trimming and for the twig decorations.

Stapler
A staple gun is indispensable for attaching fabrics to wood or board. An ordinary office stapler will secure paper, fabric and thin card (cardboard).

Stencil Card (Cardboard)
Specially made for stencilling, this card (cardboard) is coated in a water-resistant oil so that you can wipe it clean between stencils and when changing colours. Transfer your image to the card (cardboard) using a soft pencil and cut it out with a craft knife.

Tracing Paper
Another essential. When you've traced a motif you can cut it out to use as a pattern, or transfer it by rubbing the back side of the paper with a soft pencil, positioning the template, and then tracing over the outline again from the front of the paper.

cutting mat

double-sided adhesive (cellophane) tape

PVA (white) glue

staple gun

foam roller

craft knife

metal ruler

hole punch

needles

tracing paper

pins

tape measure

scissors

stapler

stencil brush

fabric marker

hot glue gun

stencil card (cardboard)

paintbrushes

plastic adhesive

ballpoint pen

pencil

permanent marker

secateurs (pruning shears)

TECHNIQUES

The projects in this book use straightforward techniques that are easy and satisfying to master. If you're doing something you haven't tried before, practise on a spare piece of fabric or paper until you're confident.

Stem Stitch

This embroidery stitch is perfect for working the outline of a design, is very simple and quick to do and creates a neat edge.

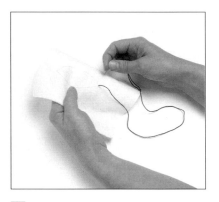

1 Cut a length of embroidery thread (floss) about 30cm (12in), thread the needle and knot the end. Bring the threaded needle up through the fabric directly through the line you have traced for the design.

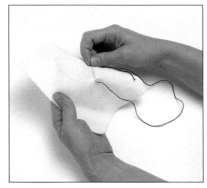

2 Put the needle back into the fabric a short way along the traced line and in the same movement bring the needle up again about halfway back towards the place where your first stitch emerged. Always keep to the traced outline.

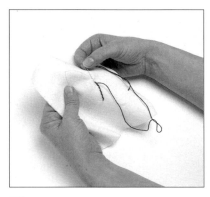

3 Put the needle into the fabric a little further along the line, making a stitch equal in length to the first. Work the whole of the outline in evenly spaced stitches, repeating step two throughout and always bringing the needle out on the same side of the previous stitch.

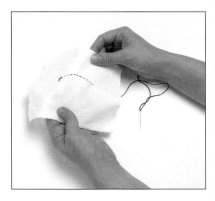

4 The back of the work will look like short running stitches.

Needlepoint Tent Stitch

This is the stitch used on canvas for needlepoint designs. When working from a chart, one square on the chart represents one intersection of the canvas. Tent stitch is usually worked horizontally.

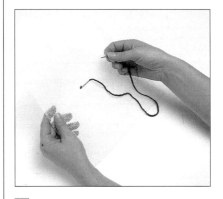

1 Cut a 45 cm (18 in) length of tapestry wool (yarn), thread the needle and knot the end. Begin with the knot on the right side of the canvas. Bring the needle up 2.5 cm (1 in) away. The first few stitches are worked over this thread to secure it. Then cut the knot off neatly.

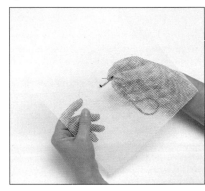

2 To work from right to left, bring your needle up through the canvas at the top left of a stitch and put it back in the square diagonally down to the right, working across one intersection of tapestry canvas.

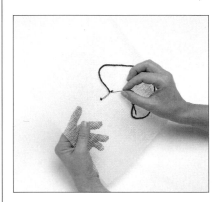

3 Bring the needle up again through the hole directly to the left of the top of the stitch you made in step two. Repeat to make a row of stitches. The stitches on the back are always longer.

4 To work from left to right, bring the needle out at the bottom of a stitch and put it back diagonally up to the left, across one intersection of canvas. All the stitches must slant in the same direction.

French Knots

French knots are used in embroidery to give a lovely raised effect. They are perfect for adding decorative detail to embroidery. To make a large French knot, use the full six strands of embroidery thread (floss).

Blanket Stitch

This stitch is traditionally used to finish the raw edges of non-fraying fabrics, such as wool and felt. It is very decorative when it is worked in a colour that contrasts with the fabric.

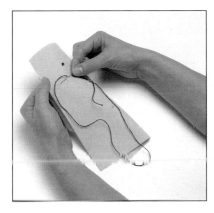

1 Thread the needle with embroidery thread (floss). Bring the needle up through the fabric at the point where you want the knot to be.

2 Make a small stitch at the same point and with the needle still in the fabric, pick up the end of the thread as it emerges from the fabric.

1 Bring the needle out from the back of the fabric a little way in from the raw edge. Insert the needle from the front to one side of the first stitch and the same distance from the edge.

2 As you pull the needle through, take it through the loop between the two stitches and gently pull up the slack. Repeat, inserting the needle from the front and pulling it through the loop.

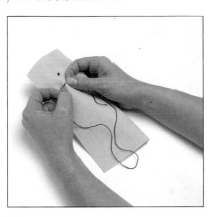

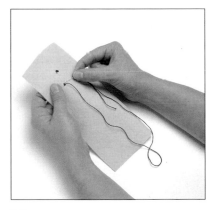

3 Wrap the thread two or three times around the needle, then pull the needle out through these threads.

4 Secure the stitch by pulling the needle back through the fabric at the point where you began the stitch.

3 To turn a corner, work three stitches into the same hole, changing the angle.

Making Templates

You may need to enlarge the templates in this book to the size you require before you use them. If you do not have access to a photocopier, follow the instructions for the grid system of enlarging templates at the back of this book

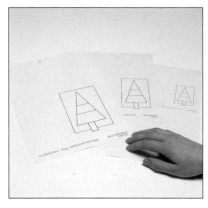 

1 Photocopy the template you are going to use, enlarging it as many times as is necessary to achieve the required correct size.

2 If you wish to use the photocopy again, or you need to trace the design on to another sheet of paper or other material, make a tracing with a soft pencil on thin plain paper or tracing paper.

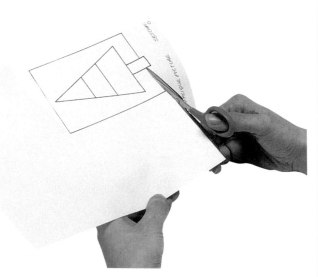

3 If you are going to use the photocopy as your template, cut it out ready to draw around. If you are working with fabric, pin the template to the fabric and draw around it lightly with tailor's chalk or a fabric marker pen.

Stencilling

Stencilling is a satisfying and easy way to produce repeated designs on paper, wood or fabric. You can cut your motif out of stencil card (cardboard) or clear acetate sheet.

1 Trace the motif on to tracing paper. Turn over and rub the back side with a soft pencil. Position the tracing face up over the stencil card (cardboard) and draw around the outline of the design.

2 Using a craft knife and cutting mat, cut the motif carefully from the card.

3 Place the stencil on the surface you wish to decorate, securing it with masking tape if necessary. Brush the paint through the stencil. Do not overload the brush: it is better to repeat the process until you achieve the desired effect, otherwise paint may bleed under the edges of the stencil. Lift off the stencil carefully.

Stamping

Stamping is great fun and so easy to do. The stamps used in this book were very simply made from thin cellulose kitchen sponge cloths, which are easy to cut into simple shapes using scissors.

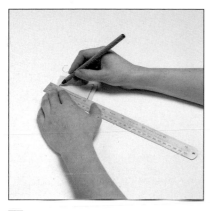

1 Draw your motif directly on to the sponge with a fine (magic) marker pen, following a paper template if necessary.

2 Cut out the motif with scissors and use a glue stick to attach it securely to a piece of corrugated cardboard.

3 Brush stencil paint directly on to the sponge, coating it well.

4 Press the stamp on to the surface to be decorated, using even pressure. Re-apply paint between each stamping to get consistent prints.

Working with Metal Foil

The aluminium and copper foil used in this book are thicker than kitchen foil, and are available from crafts suppliers. However, they are still thin enough to cut with ordinary scissors. Take great care as the edges are sharp. Use a dried-out ballpoint pen to emboss designs: this will keep the work and your hands much cleaner.

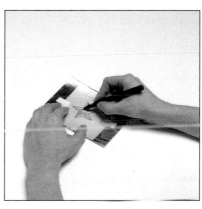

1 Position a tracing of your motif over a piece of foil and secure it with masking tape.

2 Draw the outline of the motif over the tracing paper with a ballpoint pen, pressing into the foil as you work. You can add more detail at this stage.

3 Remove the tracing paper and check the embossing, going over it again if necessary. Cut out the motif, leaving a narrow border of about 2 mm ($^1/_{16}$ in) all around the edge. Don't cut into the embossed outline.

TABLE AND MANTELPIECE DECORATIONS

Gilded Glass Spheres

With a gold glass (relief) outliner, you can turn plain glass tree decorations into unique gilded ornaments. Don't be too ambitious with your designs: you'll find that simple repeating motifs such as circles, triangles and stars are best to begin with and can be the most effective.

YOU WILL NEED
plain glass tree ornaments
white spirit (paint thinner)
gold glass (relief) outliner
paper tissues
jam jar
wire-edged ribbon
scissors

scissors

*plain glass
tree ornament*

jam jar

*gold glass
(relief)
outliner*

paper tissues

*wire-edged
ribbon*

*white
spirit (paint
thinner)*

1 Clean the glass with detergent and wipe it with white spirit (paint thinner) to remove all traces of grease.

2 Working on one side only, gently squeeze the gold glass (relief) outliner on to the glass in your chosen design. If you make a mistake, wipe the outliner off quickly with a paper tissue while it is still wet.

3 Rest the sphere in an empty jam jar and leave for about 24 hours to dry thoroughly. Decorate the other side and leave to dry again.

4 Thread a length of wire-edged ribbon through the top of the ornament and tie it in a bow.

Festive Wine Glasses

With the same gold glass (relief) outliner used to decorate the glass ornaments, you can also transform plain, everyday wine glasses. Add clear, stained-glass colours for a jewelled effect, to give your Christmas dinner the air of a medieval feast.

YOU WILL NEED
plain wine glasses
white spirit (paint thinner)
gold glass (relief) outliner
oil-based glass paints
fine paintbrush
old glass or jar
paper towel

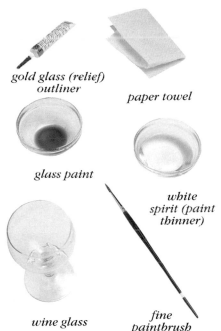

gold glass (relief) outliner

paper towel

glass paint

white spirit (paint thinner)

wine glass

fine paintbrush

1 Wash the glasses with detergent and wipe over with white spirit (paint thinner) to remove all traces of grease.

2 Pipe your design directly on to the glass with the gold outliner. Leave to dry thoroughly for at least 24 hours.

CRAFT TIP
When planning your design, it's best to avoid the rim of the glass as the relief outliner will feel bumpy against the drinker's lips. The paint colours can be mixed if you wish.

3 Check the colour and get the feel of the rather viscous glass paint by practising on an old glass or jar first. Use a fine paintbrush to colour in your design, and be careful not to get paint on the gold relief. Try to finish with each colour before changing to the next one. Clean the brush with white spirit (paint thinner) between each colour.

Gilded Christmas Plate

Seek out reasonably priced plain white plates
and turn them into glowing works of art with
ceramic paint. There's no need to reserve them
for Christmas: this crown and star design will
look lovely at any time.

YOU WILL NEED
tracing paper
pencil
carbon paper
scissors
glazed white plate, 27 cm (10½ in)
    in diameter
masking tape
oil-based ceramic paint
paintbrushes
clear polyurethane varnish

*clear
polyurethane
varnish*

*masking
tape*

ceramic paint

pencil

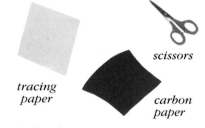

scissors

*tracing
paper*

*carbon
paper*

paintbrush

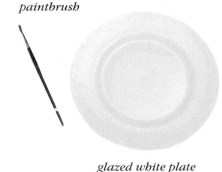

glazed white plate

1 Trace the crown, star and swirl from
the back of the book. Cut pieces of
carbon paper to the size of the tracings.

2 Starting with the crown, secure the
carbon paper and the tracing to the plate
with masking tape. Draw over the motif
to transfer it to the plate. Plan the
positions of the stars and swirls, spacing
them evenly around the rim, and transfer
them in the same way.

3 Paint in the coloured areas of the
crown and the centres of the stars and
swirls with ceramic paint, following the
manufacturer's instructions. Start at the
centre and work outwards so that your
hand does not smudge the paint. Fill in
the background with a medium brush.

4 Leave the colours to dry for about
24 hours, then paint in the gold details.
You may need two coats for a rich gold
effect. Leave to dry again for 24 hours.

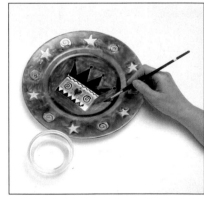

5 Cover the plate with clear varnish to
protect the surface. The decorated plate
is not suitable for food use.

Star Candle-holder

Pretty boxes, especially if they have an unusual shape, are always worth hoarding for future craft projects. This star-shaped chocolate box makes a perfect Christmas candle-holder.

YOU WILL NEED
small, rigid chocolate box with a lid
metal screw-cap from a bottle
pen
craft knife
newspaper
PVA (white) glue
paintbrush
white emulsion (latex) paint
gold (magic) marker pen
watercolour inks

PVA (white) glue

watercolour inks

bottle cap

chocolate box

pen

craft knife

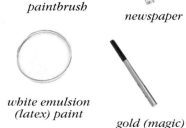

paintbrush

newspaper

white emulsion (latex) paint

gold (magic) marker pen

1 Place the bottle cap exactly in the centre of the box lid and draw around it.

2 Divide the circle into narrow pie sections and cut them with a craft knife. Fold them down into the box. Push the bottle cap into the hole so that its rim is just below the surface of the box (this will hold the candle).

3 Tear the newspaper into strips about 1 x 5 cm ($^1/_2$ x 2 in). Dilute the PVA (white) glue slightly with water. Paint a strip liberally with glue on both sides and stick it on to the box, flattening it with the paintbrush loaded with more glue. Apply a layer of newspaper all over the box in this way, beginning around the bottle cap to cover the join. Press the paper neatly over awkward corners. When the first layer is dry, apply a second and let that dry thoroughly.

4 Mix a little white emulsion (latex) paint with the glue and paint the whole box white.

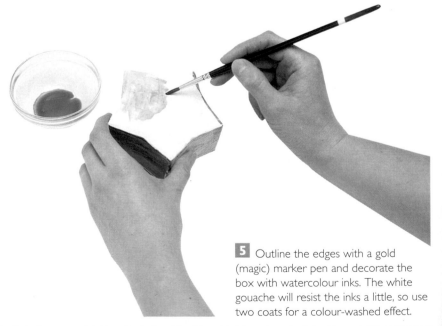

5 Outline the edges with a gold (magic) marker pen and decorate the box with watercolour inks. The white gouache will resist the inks a little, so use two coats for a colour-washed effect.

Gold Crown Tablecloth

Set the festive tone with this lovely white and gold tablecloth. The stencilling is easy and enjoyable to do, but it's important to plan your design carefully before you start work with the paint so that the motifs are evenly spaced.

YOU WILL NEED
white cotton fabric 135 cm
    (54 in) square
iron
pins
stencil card (cardboard)
craft knife
masking tape
gold stencil paint
stencil brush
fine paintbrush
sewing machine
white thread

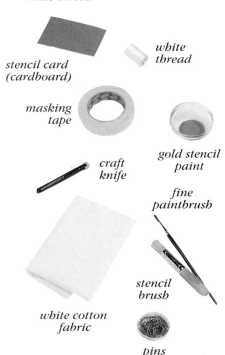

*stencil card
(cardboard)*

*white
thread*

*masking
tape*

*gold stencil
paint*

*craft
knife*

*fine
paintbrush*

*white cotton
fabric*

*stencil
brush*

pins

1 Iron the fabric to remove creases, then fold in quarters and press the folds. Fold each quarter to find the centre point, press and mark with pins. Copy the crown and shooting star templates from the back of the book, transfer on to stencil card (cardboard) and cut out with a craft knife. Stencil the crowns in the corners, then the edges and centre.

2 Stencil the shooting stars between the crowns, all pointing in the same direction around the edge of the cloth.

3 Complete the stars by touching up the gaps left by the stencil with a fine brush and gold stencil paint.

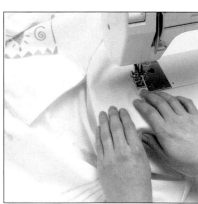

4 Press on the wrong side of the fabric to fix the paint. Hem the fabric all around the edge on a sewing machine.

CRAFT TIP
Don't overload your brush as too much paint may bleed underneath the edges of the stencil.

Holly Leaf Napkin

The Christmas table deserves something more distinctive than paper napkins, and your guests will love these specially embroidered cotton ones in festive but definitely non-traditional colours. The holly leaf motif is quick and easy to work in stem stitch.

YOU WILL NEED
paper for template
scissors
50 cm (20 in) square of washable cotton fabric in hot pink for each napkin
pins
tailor's chalk
stranded embroidery thread (floss) in acid green, acid yellow and bright orange
needle

cotton fabric   *paper*

pins

tailor's chalk

stranded embroidery thread (floss)

scissors

needle

1 Trace the holly leaf motif from the back of the book and use it to make a paper template. Pin it to one corner of the fabric, allowing room for a hem, and draw round it with tailor's chalk.

2 Using three strands of embroidery thread (floss) and working in stem stitch, embroider the outline of the holly leaf in acid green and the veins in acid yellow.

3 Fold under and pin a 5 mm (¼ in) double hem all around the napkin.

4 Using three strands of bright orange embroidery thread (floss), work a neat running stitch evenly around the hem.

Sparkling Flowerpot

This flowerpot is covered with the foil wrapped around chocolates and candies. You'll need to prepare in advance by eating plenty of foil-wrapped candies. Choose the colours carefully, and don't forget to save the wrappers! Fill the pot with baubles (balls) for a table decoration.

YOU WILL NEED
coloured foil candy wrappers
terracotta flowerpot
PVA (white) glue
paintbrush

paintbrush

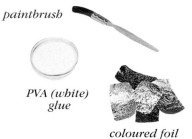

PVA (white) glue

coloured foil candy wrappers

terracotta flowerpot

1 Smooth out the coloured foils and select as many rectangular shapes as possible. If any wrappers have tears, you may be able to hide these by overlapping them with perfect pieces.

CRAFT TIP
Although you can arrange the foils in a haphazard manner for a crazy patchwork effect, this project looks best if you keep to a more regular design by placing the foil pieces horizontally and vertically.

2 Paint the flowerpot all over with PVA (white) glue to seal the surface.

3 Paint the back of a piece of foil with glue and apply it to the pot, smoothing it with the paintbrush and brushing on more glue to secure it. Continue adding the foils in an attractive pattern. When the pot is completely covered, seal it inside and out with another coat of glue.

Silver Crown Candle-holder

Masses of night-lights (tea-lights) make a lovely glowing addition to your decorative scheme: dress them up for Christmas with these easy foil crowns. Make sure the candles you buy come in their own foil pots to contain the hot wax.

YOU WILL NEED
night-light (tea-light)
heavy-gauge aluminium foil
ruler
scissors
masking tape
dried-out ballpoint pen
glue-stick

dried-out
ballpoint pen

glue-stick

masking
tape

scissors

ruler

night-light
(tea-light)

heavy-gauge
aluminium foil

1 Cut a rectangle of foil to fit around the night-light (tea-light) and overlap by about 4 cm (1½ in). The foil should stand at least 3 cm (1¼ in) higher than the night-light (tea-light).

SAFETY TIP
Never leave burning candles unattended and do not let the candle burn down to within 10 cm (2 in) of any flammable material.

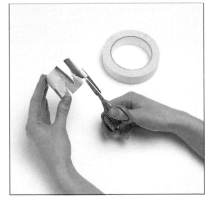

2 Wrap the foil in a circle around the candle and secure with a piece of masking tape. Cut the points of the crown freehand with scissors.

3 Remove the tape and lay the foil flat on a protected surface. Emboss a design on the foil with a dried-out ballpoint pen, making sure that it will meet neatly when the crown is joined up.

4 Roll the finished design tightly around the night-light (tea-light) to get a good candle shape and stick it together finally with a glue-stick.

Velvet Fruits

A lavish bowl full of sumptuous apples and pears in rich, fruity-coloured velvets will look like a still-life painting. You may not be able to eat them, but these fruits feel delicious!

YOU WILL NEED
paper for templates
small amounts of dress-weight velvet
    in red, plum and green
pins
scissors
sewing machine
matching thread
polyester wadding (batting)
needle

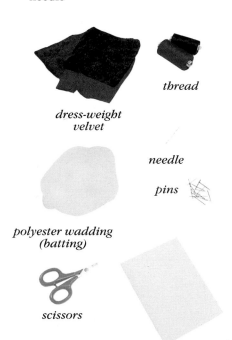

thread

dress-weight velvet

needle

pins

polyester wadding (batting)

scissors

paper

1 Trace the pear, apple and leaf shapes at the back of the book and enlarge as required. Transfer to paper and cut out the templates. Pin to the velvet and cut out, adding a 5 mm (^{1}/$_4$ in) seam allowance all round. You will need four sections for the pear and three for the apple.

CRAFT TIP

You could also use this idea to create other velvet objects on a festive theme. Why not try making some stars or holly leaves following the other templates at the back of the book?

2 With wrong sides together, pin together the side seams and machine stitch, leaving the top of the fruits open. Turn to the right side.

3 Cut two pieces of green velvet for each leaf. Machine stitch together, leaving the end open, and turn to the right side. Gather the end with a needle and thread to give a realistic leaf shape.

4 Stuff each fruit with polyester wadding (batting). Sew up the opening at the top with a needle and thread, catching in the leaf as you sew.

White Christmas Tree

Stand this abstract, modern interpretation of the traditional star-topped Christmas tree on a side-table or the mantelpiece. It looks best as part of a cool, monochrome arrangement in white or gold.

YOU WILL NEED
hot glue gun
coarse sisal (parcel) string
large polystyrene cone
scissors
small polystyrene star
white emulsion (latex) paint
paintbrush
gold paint

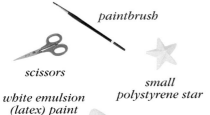

paintbrush

scissors

white emulsion (latex) paint

small polystyrene star

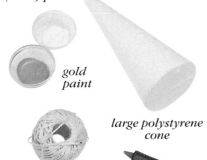

gold paint

large polystyrene cone

coarse sisal (parcel) string

hot glue gun

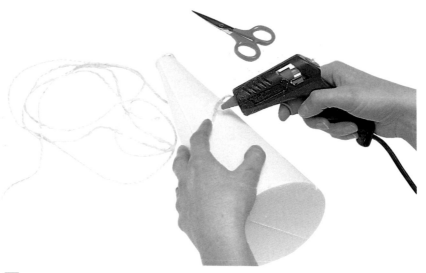

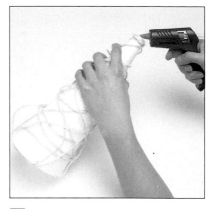

2 Wind a short length of string in a coil and glue it to the top of the cone for the star to sit on.

1 With a hot glue gun, attach the end of the string to the base of the cone. Wind the string up the cone towards the point, then down to the base again, gluing it as you work and securing it when it crosses. Each time you reach the base, cut the string and start again from another point so that the cone is evenly covered.

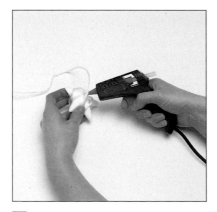

CRAFT TIP

Make sure the ends of the string are evenly spaced around the base of the cone so that it stands upright.

3 Wind and glue string around the star in the same way. Hide the raw ends under the string. Glue the star to the top of the cone.

4 Paint the cone and star with several coats of white emulsion (latex) paint, covering the string and filling in any unsightly dents in the polystyrene.

5 Finish by brushing roughly over the string with gold paint.

Silk-wrapped Candle Pot

Here's a simple way to incorporate a beautiful piece of silk in to your decorative scheme. Match all the rich colours of the fabric when you are choosing the candles. Play safe with candles and never leave them burning unattended.

YOU WILL NEED
terracotta flowerpot
corrugated cardboard
gold paper
marker pen
scissors
double-sided adhesive
  (cellophane) tape
square of silk fabric to fit
  comfortably around the pot
newspaper or tissue paper
selection of coloured candles in
  various sizes
plastic adhesive

gold paper   *plastic adhesive*

corrugated cardboard

candles

square of silk fabric

scissors

marker pen

newspaper

terracotta flowerpot

1 Try out the candles in the flowerpot to find a suitable height at which they should stand. Cut out a circle of cardboard to fit in the pot at this level as a base for the candles.

2 Cut a larger circle of gold paper and use it to cover the cardboard. Fold the edges under neatly and secure with double-sided adhesive (cellophane) tape.

3 Neaten the edges of the silk and stand the flowerpot in the centre of the square. Take two opposite corners and bring them up over the sides of the pot, tucking them inside. Tie the other two corners together at the front and arrange the folds of the silk in a pleasing manner.

4 Pad the base of the pot firmly with newspaper or tissue paper then place the gold disc inside. Arrange the candles on the disc, then secure them with small pieces of plastic adhesive.

Willow Twig Napkin Rings

You can decorate with natural, homespun materials but still achieve a sparkling effect if you choose bright, glowing colours. Using glue to assemble these rings reinforces the fabric and is a welcome short-cut if making a large quantity.

YOU WILL NEED
willow twigs
secateurs (pruning shears)
11 x 22 cm (4¼ x 8½ in) coarsely woven cotton fabric per ring
fabric glue
paintbrush
stranded embroidery thread (floss)
needle
scissors
pins
matching thread

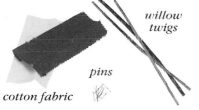

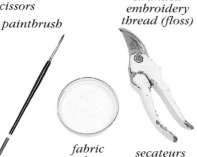

cotton fabric

willow twigs

pins

needle

thread

scissors

paintbrush

stranded embroidery thread (floss)

fabric glue

secateurs (pruning shears)

1 Cut four pieces of twig, each 9 cm (3½ in) long.

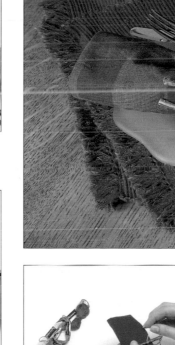

2 Make a 1 cm (½ in) hem along one short end of the fabric and glue it down. Fold the long sides of the fabric rectangle to the centre and glue.

3 Position the twigs evenly across the centre of the right side of the fabric. Using three strands of embroidery thread (floss) oversew the twigs on to the napkin ring.

4 Pin the ends of the ring together, tucking the raw edge into the folded edge. Slip-stitch together.

The Christmas Mantelpiece

In restrained tones of cream and green, this elegant arrangement concentrates on contrasting shapes and textures. Placing it in front of a mirror makes it doubly effective. The key to success is scale: use the largest-leaved ivy and the thickest candles you can find to make a really stylish design statement.

YOU WILL NEED
polystyrene balls
double-sided adhesive (cellophane) tape
scissors
reindeer moss
ivory candles of various heights and widths
foil dishes (for baking or take-out food)
plastic adhesive
stems of ivy
florist's wire

florist's wire *scissors*

foil dish *ivory candle*

plastic adhesive *polystyrene ball* *ivy*

double-sided adhesive (cellophane) tape

reindeer moss

1 To make the moss balls, cover the polystyrene shapes all over with double-sided adhesive (cellophane) tape.

2 Press the moss gently on to the balls, covering well so that none of the polystyrene can be seen.

3 Arrange the candles on foil dishes, to protect the mantelpiece from hot, dripping wax. Secure the candles in the dishes with pieces of plastic adhesive.

4 Wire together small bunches of ivy and attach them to a longer main stem to make a lush garland. Arrange the candles on the mantelpiece and drape the garlands in front of them. Position the moss balls around the candles.

SAFETY TIP
Never leave burning candles unattended and do not allow the candle to burn down to within 5cm (2in) of the foliage or other decoration materials.

Christmas Crackers

Making your own Christmas crackers is really rewarding and it's great fun watching friends and family pull them open to discover the treats inside. Make exactly the number you need for your party and collect small gifts to put in them.

YOU WILL NEED
double-sided crepe paper in
    bright colours
craft knife
metal ruler
cutting mat
thin card (cardboard) in black
    and white
double-sided adhesive
    (cellophane) tape
cracker snaps
paper hats, jokes and gifts to
    go in the crackers
narrow black ribbon
gold paper-backed foil
corrugated cardboard
gold crepe paper
fine gold cord

metal ruler

craft knife

cracker snaps

double-sided crepe paper

gold crepe paper

fine gold cord

narrow black ribbon

gold paper-backed foil

thin card (cardboard)

paper hats, jokes and gifts

double-sided adhesive (cellophane) tape

1 For each cracker, cut two rectangles of crepe paper measuring 25 × 20 cm (10 × 8 in). Join, overlapping the ends, to make a rectangle 45 × 20 cm (18 × 8 in).

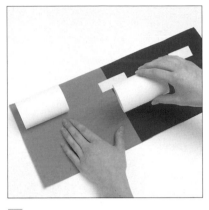

2 Cut three pieces of thin white card (cardboard) 22 × 10 cm (9 × 4 in). Roll each into a cylinder, overlapping the short ends by 3.5 cm (1¼ in). Lay strips of double-sided adhesive (cellophane) tape across the crepe paper with which to attach the card cylinders: one in the centre and the other two about 4 cm (1½ in) in from each end of the rectangle. Roll up and secure the edge with double-sided tape.

3 Decorate the cracker with strips of the gold papers. To make the corrugated paper, lay a strip of paper-backed foil over a piece of corrugated cardboard and ease the foil into the ridges with your thumb. Cut a simple star shape out of thin black card (cardboard), wrap some fine gold cord around it and stick it on top of the gold decorations (use one of the star templates at the back of the book or draw your own).

4 Insert the snap and place the novelties and a paper hat in the central section of the cracker.

5 Tie up the ends with narrow black ribbon, easing the crepe paper gently so that you can tie the knots very tightly.

6 Complete the cracker by folding the edges of the crepe paper over the ends of the cardboard cylinders.

Citrus Centrepiece

Perhaps because they're at their best at this time of year, oranges feature in many traditional Christmas recipes and their warm spicy smell readily evokes the festive season. A sparkling glass bowl of citrus fruits brings a flash of sunshine into the house in the depths of winter and makes a glowing, fragrant centrepiece.

CRAFT TIP

If you are using a lino-cutting tool for this project, paint the blade with a coat of clear nail varnish to prevent it discolouring the fruit.

YOU WILL NEED

oranges, lemons and limes
V-shaped lino-cutting tool or
    canelle knife
sharp knife
wire-edged ribbon
scissors
florist's stub (floral) wire
glass dish or bowl
sprigs of fresh bay leaves
secateurs (pruning shears)

sharp knife

glass bowl

citrus fruits

florist's stub (floral) wire

scissors

wire-edged ribbon

V-shaped lino-cutting tool

fresh bay leaves

secateurs (pruning shears)

1 Use the lino-cutting tool or canelle knife to cut grooves in the peel of the fruits and reveal the white pith beneath. Follow the contours of the fruit in a spiral or make straight cuts.

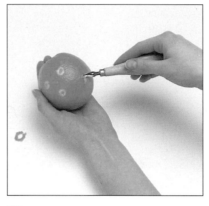

2 On other fruits, try making an overall pattern of small circles. Practise the patterns on spare fruits you intend to cook with or eat.

3 With a very sharp knife, cut thin spirals of orange peel as long as possible to drape over the arrangement.

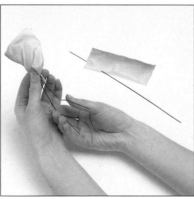

4 Cut short lengths of wire-edged ribbon, fold into loops and secure the ends with florist's stub (floral) wire.

5 Arrange the fruits in your chosen container, tucking in the ribbon loops and adding a few sprigs of fresh green bay leaves.

Silk Purses

Ribbons are available in a great range of widths and colours and you need only a small amount of each to make these delicate little purses to hang on your tree. Use luxurious satins or sheer organza (organdy), with contrasting colours for generous bows around the top.

YOU WILL NEED
an assortment of ribbons
scissors
pins
matching thread
needle
fine gold cord
polyester wadding (batting)

needle

thread

polyester wadding (batting)

pins

fine gold cord

scissors

ribbons

1 Cut enough ribbon to make a pleasing purse shape when folded in two, short sides together, allowing for the raw edges to be folded down at the top. To make a striped purse, pin and stitch three narrower lengths together using running stitch.

2 With the wrong sides together, sew up the sides of the purse by hand, or using a sewing machine if you prefer.

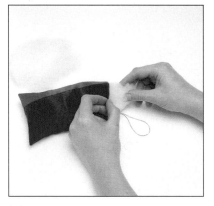

3 Turn the purse right side out and tuck the raw edges inside. Stitch on a loop of fine gold cord for hanging. Stuff lightly with polyester wadding (batting).

4 Gather the top of the purse together and tie with another piece of ribbon, finishing with a pretty bow.

Victorian Boots

Use the richest fabrics you can find to make these delicate boots: fine raw silks and taffetas in glowing colours are perfect. The two sides of the decoration should harmonize well.

YOU WILL NEED
thin white card (cardboard)
pencil
stapler
scissors
scraps of fabric
fabric glue
paintbrush
fine gold cord

scraps of fabric
fine gold cord
scissors
pencil
thin white card (cardboard)
fabric glue
paintbrush
stapler

1 Trace the boot motif from the back of the book and transfer it on to thin card (cardboard). Fold the card in two and staple the layers together at the edges so that you can cut out two exactly matching templates. Cut the boots out with scissors.

2 Separate the templates. Turn one over and glue each on to a piece of coordinating fabric.

3 Cut around each boot leaving an allowance of barely 1 cm ($\frac{1}{2}$ in). Snip the excess fabric around all the curves and stick down firmly to the back of the card.

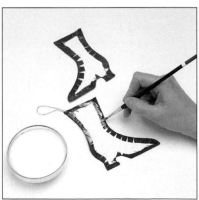

4 Glue a loop of cord to the back of one card for hanging, then glue the two sides of the boot together and leave to dry thoroughly.

Glitter Keys

A simple idea for transforming everyday objects into fantasy tree decorations. Once you've picked up the glitter habit, you may find you want to cover all kinds of other things – and why not?

YOU WILL NEED
old keys in various shapes and sizes
PVA (white) glue
old paintbrush
sheets of scrap paper
coloured glitter
fine gold cord

old paintbrush

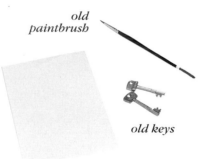
scrap paper

old keys

coloured glitter

PVA (white) glue

fine gold cord

1 Using an old paintbrush, cover one side of the key with a coat of undiluted PVA (white) glue.

2 Lay the key on a sheet of scrap paper and sprinkle generously with glitter. Repeat with the other keys, using a separate sheet of paper for each one. Allow to dry completely.

3 Remove the key. Pinch the paper to make a groove for the spare glitter to run into. Pour it back into the container. Glue the remaining areas of the keys and repeat the process. Add further layers to build up quite a thick coating. Tie a loop of gold cord to each key for hanging.

CRAFT TIP

PVA (white) glue dries to a transparent glaze, so you can brush it on over glitter you have already applied when building up the layers on the keys.

Ornamental Keys

Gold paint and fake gems can turn a bunch of old keys into something truly wonderful – fit to unlock a fairy-tale castle or treasure chest.

YOU WILL NEED
old keys in assorted shapes and
    sizes
gold spray paint
gold braid
hot glue gun
flat-backed fake gems in
    assorted colours

*gold spray
paint*

scissors

gold braid

old keys

*flat-backed
fake gems*

hot glue gun

1 Make sure the keys are free of rust. Working with one side at a time, spray with gold paint and allow to dry.

2 Cut the gold braid to a suitable length for hanging the key. Fold in half and attach the ends to the key with the hot glue gun

3 Cover the ends of the braid by gluing a jewel over them. Arrange two or three more jewels on the key and glue them on. Allow to dry thoroughly.

Carnival Mask

A stunning decoration inspired by the traditional costume of the masked Harlequin. Use the fragile foil from candy wrappers for part of the design to mimic the expensive look of fine gold leaf.

YOU WILL NEED
tracing paper
thin white card (cardboard)
scissors
craft knife
pencil
ruler
metallic crayons in gold and lilac
glitter paint
PVA (white) glue
glitter
foil candy wrappers
sequins
gold doily
matt gold paper
glue-stick
fine gold cord
gold button

matt gold paper
sequins
PVA (white) glue
gold doily
glitter paint
glitter brush
thin white card (cardboard)
metallic crayons
pencil
ruler
craft knife
fine gold cord
scissors
glue-stick
gold button
candy wrappers

1 Trace the template from the back of the book and transfer it to thin white card (cardboard). Cut out the mask shape and eye holes. Use a soft pencil to draw in the diagonals for the diamonds.

2 Decorate the diamond shapes in different colours and textures. Use metallic crayons, adding glitter paint on some for texture. Paint PVA (white) glue on to others and sprinkle with glitter. When dry, coat thinly with more glue to fix the glitter. Cut diamonds from the candy wrappers and glue these on last to cover any rough edges.

3 Trim the eye holes with rows of gold sequins and the edging cut from a gold doily.

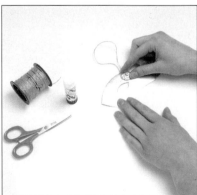

4 Use the template to cut a second mask shape from matt gold paper. Glue this to the back of your mask. Attach a loop of fine gold cord for hanging, covering the ends with a gold button.

Lacy Silver Gloves

Dainty Victorian ladies' gloves make a pretty motif for a traditional glittering tree ornament. Use translucent glass paints, which adhere well and let the foil shine through the colour.

YOU WILL NEED
tracing paper
heavy-gauge aluminium foil
masking tape
dried-out ballpoint pen
scissors
oil-based glass paints
paintbrush
fine gold cord

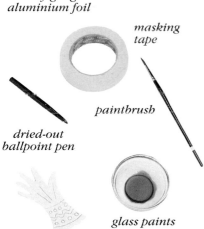

fine gold cord

scissors

heavy-gauge aluminium foil

masking tape

paintbrush

dried-out ballpoint pen

glass paints

tracing paper

1 Trace the template from the back of the book and attach the tracing to a piece of foil with masking tape. Draw over the design to transfer it to the foil. Remove the tracing and complete the embossing with an old ballpoint pen.

2 Cut out the glove, leaving a narrow border of about 2 mm (¹/₁₆ in) all around the edge: don't cut into the embossed outline. Make a hole in one corner of the glove with the point of the scissors.

3 Paint the design with glass paints, keeping the colours within the embossed outlines. Allow to dry completely for at least 24 hours.

4 Thread a loop of fine gold cord through the hole for hanging.

Gilded Rosettes

These flower-like ornaments can be hung on the tree or used to decorate a sumptuously wrapped gift for someone special. Gold lamé makes an opulent setting for an ornate gilt button, but ring the changes with luxurious velvets too.

YOU WILL NEED
paper for template
pencil
small pieces of silk, lamé or dress-
    weight velvet
pins
scissors
matching thread
needle
fine gold cord
ornate buttons
hot glue gun

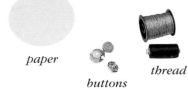

lamé and silk   *fine gold cord*

paper

buttons   *thread*

pins   *needle*

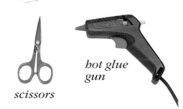

scissors   *hot glue gun*

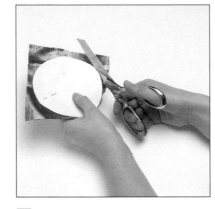

1 Draw and cut out a circular template about 12 cm (5 in) in diameter, pin to a single layer of fabric and cut out (there is no need for a seam allowance).

2 Using double thread, sew in running stitch all round the circle 5 mm (¹/₄ in) from the edge. Pull the thread taut to form the rosette and secure the ends.

3 Thread a loop of fine gold cord through the top of the rosette for hanging the decoration.

4 Using a hot glue gun, attach a button in the centre to cover the raw edges.

Exotic Ornaments

These sequinned and beaded balls look like a collection of priceless Fabergé treasures, yet they're simple and fun to make. Hang them on the tree or pile them in a dish for a show-stopping decoration.

YOU WILL NEED
silky covered polystyrene balls
paper for template
pins
gold netting
scissors
double-sided adhesive
    (cellophane) tape
gold braid
sequins in a variety of shapes
    and colours
small glass and pearl beads
brass-headed pins, 1 cm (½ in) long

scissors

sequins

gold netting

small beads

gold braid

paper

double-sided adhesive (cellophane) tape

silky covered polystyrene ball

pins

brass-headed pins

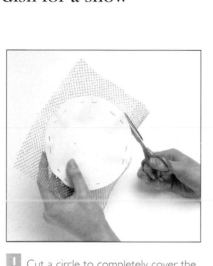

1 Cut a circle to completely cover the ball and make a paper template. Pin to the gold netting and cut out.

2 Secure the netting to the ball using tiny pieces of double-sided adhesive (cellophane) tape. The tape and raw edges will be hidden later with sequins.

3 For an alternative design cut lengths of gold braid and pin around the ball to make a framework for your sequins.

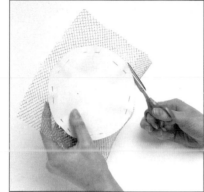

4 Attach a loop of gold thread to the ball with a brass-headed pin. Thread a bead and sequin on to a brass-headed pin and gently press into the ball. Repeat until each design is complete.

CRAFT TIP

Silk-covered balls are available as ready-made tree ornaments. When you are working out your designs, use simple repeating patterns and avoid using too many colours on each one, since this can look too busy.

Cookies for the Tree

Use your favourite gingerbread cookie recipe to make some delicious edible decorations. If you'd rather they didn't all disappear from the tree almost before Christmas has begun, you can dry them right out in the oven. Either way, don't forget to make a small hole at the top of each cookie while they're still warm so that you can hang them up.

YOU WILL NEED
rolling pin
gingerbread cookie dough
a festive assortment of cookie
    cutters
skewer
garden twine
scraps of homespun check fabric

skewer

check fabric

garden twine　*scissors*

cookie cutter　*gingerbread
cookie dough*

rolling pin

1 Roll out the cookie dough to a thickness of about 1 cm (¹/₂ in).

2 Gently cut out your chosen shapes with cookie cutters. Bake the cookies in batches according to the recipe.

3 While the cookies are still warm from the oven, carefully pierce a small hole in the top of each one with a skewer. If the cookies are not intended for eating, return them to the lowest shelf of a very low oven to allow them to dry out thoroughly.

4 Thread a loop of garden twine through each hole. Cut a small strip of homespun fabric and tie this around the loop of twine to finish the decoration.

Button Garland

An assortment of old buttons can be given new life as an original garland for the Christmas tree. Use fairly large ones for this project: save your little shirt buttons for other decorative ornament

YOU WILL NEED
an assortment of buttons
garden twine
scissors
hot glue gun

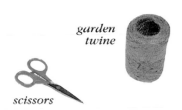

garden twine

scissors

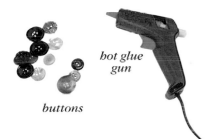

hot glue gun

buttons

1 Spread all your buttons out so that you can choose a variety of colours and sizes. Balance the weight of the buttons by using small ones with larger ones, and choose a pleasing combination of colours to go along the garland

2 Heat the hot glue gun and put a dot of glue on the back of a button. Lay the twine on top and wait a few seconds for the glue to harden.

SAFETY TIP
Take care with your fingers when using the hot glue gun as hot glue may squeeze through the holes in the buttons and cause a burn.

3 Glue a second button on the other side of the twine. Glue buttons all along the string in the same way, spacing them evenly. The length of your garland will depend on the size of your tree and the number of buttons you have.

A Country Angel

This endearing character, with her homespun clothes and tightly knotted hair, is bound to be a friend for many Christmases to come.

YOU WILL NEED

40 x 24 cm- (16 x 10 in-) piece natural calico

40 x 26 cm- (16 x 10 ¼ in-) piece check cotton homespun or small-scale gingham

30 x 22 cm (12 x 9 in)-piece blue and white ticking

tea

paper for templates

scissors

fabric marker pen

sewing machine

matching thread

polyester wadding (batting)

twigs

secateurs (pruning shears)

fine permanent (magic) marker

stranded embroidery thread (floss) in brown

needle

garden twine

scrap of red woollen fabric

fabric stiffener (starch)

copper wire

all-purpose glue

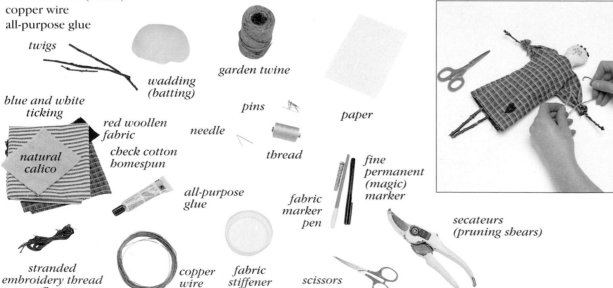

twigs

wadding (batting)

garden twine

blue and white ticking

red woollen fabric

pins

paper

natural calico

check cotton homespun

needle

thread

all-purpose glue

fine permanent (magic) marker

fabric marker pen

stranded embroidery thread (floss)

copper wire

fabric stiffener (starch)

scissors

secateurs (pruning shears)

1 Begin by washing all the fabrics to remove any chemicals. While they are still damp, soak them in tea. Don't worry if the colouring is uneven as this adds to their rustic, aged appearance. Trace the patterns for the head, dress and wings from the back of the book. Cut the head and torso out of doubled calico, leaving a 1 cm (½ in) seam allowance.

2 Machine stitch the two body pieces right sides together leaving the lower edge open. Clip the curves and turn to the right side. Stuff softly with polyester wadding (batting). Cut two twigs about 20 cm (8 in) long and stick them into the body to make the legs. Sew up the opening, securing the legs as you go.

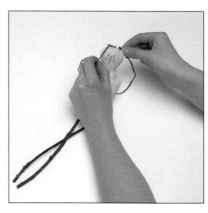

3 With a very fine permanent (magic) marker, draw the eyes, nose and mouth on to the face. Make heavy French knots with embroidery thread around the top of the face for the hair.

4 Use the paper pattern to cut out the dress from the check fabric. Sew up the sides, leaving the sleeves and hem with raw edges. Cut a slit in the top for the neck and turn the dress to the right side. Cut a small heart from the red woollen fabric and attach to the dress with a single cross stitch in brown embroidery thread (floss). Put the dress on the angel, then place short twigs inside the sleeves, securing them tightly at the wrists with garden twine. The twigs should be short enough to let the arms bend forwards.

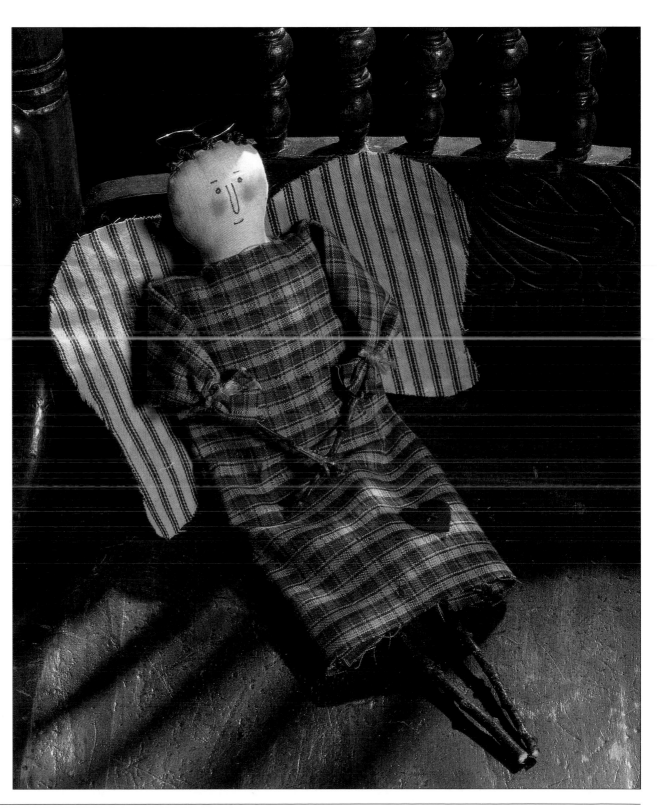

5 Cut the wings out of the ticking and fray the raw edges slightly. Apply fabric stiffener (starch) liberally to the wings to soak them thoroughly. Lay them completely flat to dry.

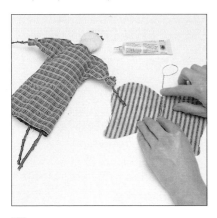

6 Make a halo from copper wire, leaving a long end to glue to the wings. Stitch the wings securely to the back of the body through the dress.

Raffia Balls

Here's another idea to decorate the natural Christmas tree. Instead of glitzy glass ornaments, hang up these little balls covered in creamy, undyed raffia. Their subtle shade and interesting texture go really beautifully with the tree's soft green branches.

YOU WILL NEED
fine copper wire
scissors
small polystyrene balls
double-sided adhesive (cellophane) tape
natural (garden) raffia

natural (garden) raffia

fine copper wire

small polystyrene ball

scissors

double-sided adhesive (cellophane) tape

 1 Cut a short piece of wire and make it into a loop. Stick the ends into a polystyrene ball.

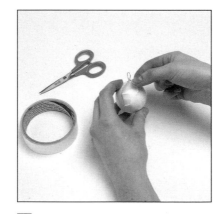

2 Cover the ball completely in double-sided adhesive (cellophane) tape.

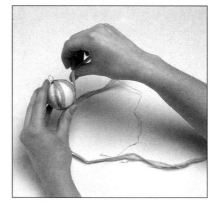

3 Arrange the hank of raffia so that you can remove lengths without tangling them. Holding the first 10 cm (4 in) of the strand at the top of the ball, wind the raffia around the ball working from top to bottom and covering it as evenly as possible.

4 When you have finished covering the ball, tie the end of the raffia to the length you left free at the beginning. Using a few lengths of raffia together, form a loop with which to hang the decoration and finish with a bow.

CRAFT TIP

As an alternative, try using coloured raffia for a more varied effect.

Twiggy Stars

Buy a bundle of willow twigs or, better still, hunt for them in winter woods and gardens. These pretty stars would look equally effective hanging on the tree or in a window.

YOU WILL NEED
willow twigs
secateurs (pruning shears)
stranded embroidery thread (floss)
checked cotton fabric
scissors
natural (garden) raffia

willow twigs

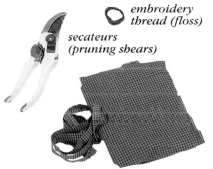
natural (garden) raffia   *scissors*

embroidery thread (floss)

secateurs (pruning shears)

checked cotton fabric

1 Cut the twigs into lengths of 15 cm (6 in) using the secateurs (pruning shears. You will need five for each star.

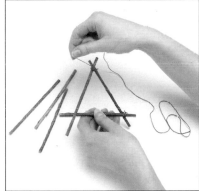

2 Tie the first pair of twigs together near the ends with a length of embroidery thread (floss), winding it around and between to form a "V" shape. Repeat with the remaining twigs, arranging them under and over each other as shown in the photograph to form a five-pointed star.

3 Cut the fabric into strips approximately 15 x 2 cm (6 x ¾ in).

4 Tie a length of fabric in a double knot over the thread securing each point of the star. Attach a loop of raffia to hang the decoration.

Tiny Knitted Socks

Miniature socks would be a charming addition to the tree, especially appropriate for a baby's first Christmas. They're lightly stuffed with wadding (batting), but if you prefer you could wrap up a tiny present to peep out of the top.

ABBREVIATIONS

K: knit; P: purl; st: stitch; Sl: slip st from one needle to the other; psso: pass the slipped stitch over the one just worked; K2 tog: pick up two stitches and knit them together.

YOU WILL NEED

4-ply knitting yarn in off-white
set of four double-ended knitting needles in a size suitable for your yarn
polyester wadding (batting)
needle

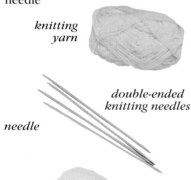

knitting yarn

double-ended knitting needles

needle

polyester wadding (batting)

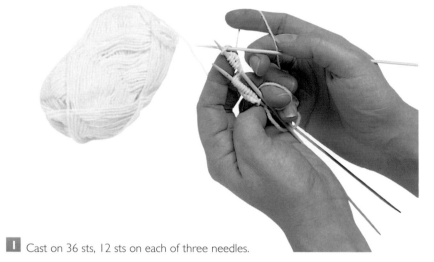

1 Cast on 36 sts, 12 sts on each of three needles.

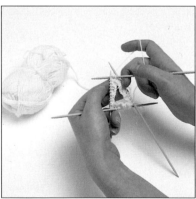

2 Work rib of K2, P2 for 2.5 cm (1 in).

3 Work a further 5.5 cm (2¼ in) in stocking stitch. Shape the heel: knit 10 rows in stocking stitch on one set of 12 sts only. Continuing on these 12 sts only, K3, Sl1, K1, psso, K2, K2 tog, K3, turn and P back. Next row: K2, Sl1, K1, psso, K2, K2 tog, K2, turn and P back. Next row: K1, Sl1, K1, psso, K2, K2 tog, K1. Turn and P back. Next row: K1, Sl1, K1, psso, K2 tog, K1. This leaves 4 sts on the needle.

4 Turn the heel: pick up 10 sts along each side of the heel and arrange 16 sts on each needle with one division at the centre of the heel just worked: this will be the beginning of the round. Now work around the whole sock in continuous rows. 1st round: K13, K2 tog, K1; K1, Sl1, K1, psso, K10, K2 tog, K1; K1, Sl1, K1, psso, K13. 2nd round: K12, K2 tog,K1; K1, Sl1, K1, psso, K8, K2 tog, K1; K1, Sl1, K1, psso, K12. 3rd round: K11, K2 tog, K1; K1, Sl1, K1, psso, K6, K2 tog, K1; K1, Sl1, K1, psso, K11. 4th round: K10, K2 tog, K1; K10; K1, Sl1, K1, psso, K10.

Work 22 plain rounds in K for foot.

Shape the toe: 1st round: K1, Sl1, K1 psso, K6, K2 tog, K1 (12 sts); K1, Sl1, K1, psso, K4, K2 tog, K1 (10 sts); K1, Sl1, K1, psso, K6, K2 tog, K1 (12 sts). 2nd round: K1, Sl1, K1, psso, K4, K2 tog, K1 (10 sts); K1, Sl1, K1, psso, K2, K2 tog, K1 (8 sts); K1, Sl1, K1, psso, K4, K2 tog, K1 (10 sts). 3rd round: K1, Sl1, K1, psso, K2, K2 tog, K1 (8 sts); K1, Sl1, K1, psso, K2, K2 tog, K1 (8 sts); K1, Sl1, K1, psso, K2, K2 tog, K1 (8 sts). 4th round: K1, Sl1, K1, psso, K1, K2 tog, K1 (7 sts); K1, Sl1, K1, psso, K1, K2 tog, K1 (7 sts); K1, Sl1, K1, psso, K1, K2 tog, K1 (7 sts).

5 Break off the wool, thread all the remaining stitches on it, draw up and fasten securely. Press gently using steam and pad lightly with polyester wadding (batting). Make a loop at the top for hanging, using the cast on end.

CRAFT TIP

Try to keep an even tension when knitting. Don't pull the yarn too tightly around the needles or the work will start to pucker.

Pearl Houses and Hearts

Almost everyone has a collection of little creamy-white buttons that can be turned into these lovely pearly tree decorations. Try to include some real mother-of-pearl buttons, which have a beautiful sheen and interesting tonal variations.

YOU WILL NEED
paper for template
scissors
plain corrugated cardboard
pencil
masking tape
craft knife
garden twine
hot glue gun
selection of mother-of-pearl and
    plastic buttons in various sizes

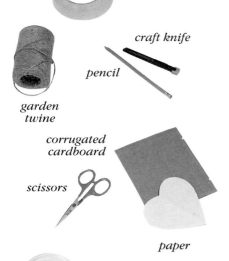

masking tape

craft knife

pencil

garden twine

corrugated cardboard

scissors

paper

buttons

hot glue gun

1 Make paper templates for the house and heart and secure them to the corrugated cardboard with masking tape. Draw around the templates.

2 Cut out the shapes using a craft knife. Cut a short length of garden twine and glue it in a loop at the top of the ornament with the glue gun.

3 Arrange the buttons all over the shapes, covering them completely. Choose different sizes to fit neatly together. When you are happy with your arrangement, attach the buttons individually with the hot glue gun.

4 On the back of each decoration, conceal the ends of the twine by gluing a button over them.

Warm Woolly Heart

A plump, soft heart edged in bold blanket-stitch will make an original addition to your rustic tree. Subtly coordinated fabrics give prominence to its unusual textures – everyone will want to touch it.

YOU WILL NEED
paper for template
scraps of two coordinating woollen
    fabrics
scissors
polyester wadding (batting)
pins
contrasting stranded embroidery
    thread (floss)
needle
garden twine

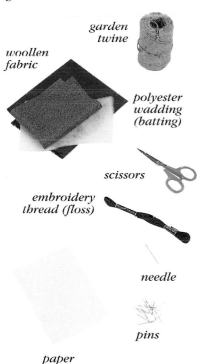

garden twine

woollen fabric

polyester wadding (batting)

scissors

embroidery thread (floss)

needle

pins

paper

CRAFT TIP

Cut out the appliqué cross freehand. It doesn't matter if the strips are not exactly true: this will add to the heart's rustic appearance.

1 Trace the template from the back of the book and use it to cut out two hearts, one from each fabric. Cut two small strips for the appliqué cross. Use the template again to cut out a piece of wadding (batting), then trim off about 1 cm (½ in) all round the edge.

2 Pin the cross pieces on the contrasting fabric and attach with large oversewing stitches, using three strands of embroidery thread (floss).

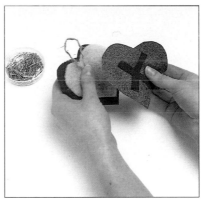

3 Pin all the layers together, sandwiching the wadding between the fabric hearts. Make a loop of twine for hanging the ornament and insert the ends in the top.

4 Stitch all around the edges in blanket stitch with three strands of embroidery thread (floss). Make sure the twine is secured as you go.

Santa's Toy Sack

Leave this gorgeous sack by the fireplace on Christmas Eve and Santa's guaranteed to fill it. Alternatively, it would be a wonderful way to deliver all your gifts if you're visiting friends. The contrast in texture between the luxurious satin ribbons and the coarse weave of the sack is novel and effective.

YOU WILL NEED

1.6 x 1.1 m (63 x 43 in) hessian
    (burlap), washed
tape measure
scissors
pins
sewing machine
selection of contrasting satin
    ribbons, 3.5 – 4.5 cm
    (1¼ – 1¾ in) wide
bodkin or safety pin
matching thread
needle

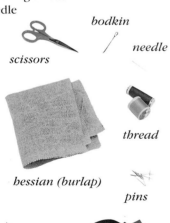

scissors   *bodkin*

                    needle

hessian (burlap)   *thread*

                    pins

tape measure   *satin ribbons*

1 Trim the washed hessian (burlap) so that it measures 1 x 1.5 m (39 x 59 in). Fold it in half, right sides together, bringing the shorter sides together, and pin across the bottom and up the side, making a seam allowance of approximately 4 cm (1½ in).

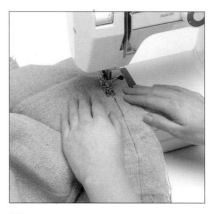

2 Machine stitch the bottom and one side of the sack.

4 With a bodkin, or safety pin, thread a length of contrasting ribbon through the channel you have created. Make sure it is long enough to make a generous bow when the top of the sack is gathered up. Turn the sack right side out.

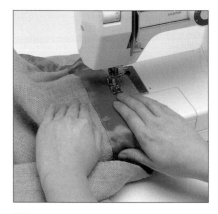

3 Still working on the wrong side, turn down the top edge by approximately 7 cm (3 in). Pin, then cover the raw edge with a length of satin ribbon. Fold under the raw ends of the ribbon to leave an opening. Machine stitch close to the top and bottom edges of the ribbon.

5 Using a double thread, stitch along one edge of a length of ribbon in running stitch. Draw the ribbon up into gathers. Cut to length allowing for joining the ends, flatten out and measure how much you need to make a rosette. Then cut all the ribbons to this length. Gather again and secure tightly, joining the raw edges invisibly from the wrong side.

6 Make enough rosettes in assorted colours to make a pleasing arrangement on the front of the sack. Stitch on the rosettes by hand.

CRAFT TIP

Hessian (burlap) is not pre-shrunk, so wash the fabric before you begin to make the sack. Use your machine's hottest setting, then press with a steam iron or damp cloth to remove all the creases.

Appliqué Christmas Tree

A charmingly simple little picture which you can frame or mount on card (cardboard) as a seasonal greeting for a special person. Contrasting textures in the homespun fabrics and simple, childlike stitches give it a naïve appeal.

YOU WILL NEED
scraps of homespun fabrics in
  greens, red and orange
scissors
matching thread
needle
coarse off-white cotton
pins
stranded embroidery thread (floss)
gold embroidery thread (floss)
iron
picture frame

gold embroidery thread (floss)

embroidery thread (floss)

thread

scissors

coarse off-white cotton

scraps of homespun fabrics

needle

pins

1 Following the template at the back of the book, cut out the pieces for the Christmas tree from three different shades and textures of green fabric. Cut out a red rectangle for the background and an orange stem. Join the three sections of the tree with running stitches.

2 Pin all the pieces to a backing of off-white cotton large enough to fill your picture frame.

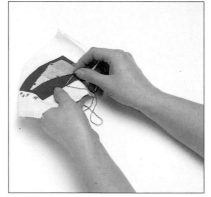

3 Sew the pieces together invisibly in slip-stitch, tucking the edges under with your needle as you sew. Aim for a slightly uneven, naïve appearance. Add gold stars and coloured stitch details using three strands of embroidery thread (floss). Press gently before framing.

Heavenly Gold Star

Collect as many different kinds of gold paper as you can find to cover this sparkling star with its subtle variations of texture. It makes a lovely wall or mantelpiece decoration, and would look equally splendid at the top of the tree.

YOU WILL NEED
assorted gold paper: candy
    wrappers, metallic crepe paper,
    gift-wrap etc
polystyrene star
fine wire
scissors
masking tape
PVA (white) glue
paintbrush
gold glitter paint

paintbrush

masking tape

PVA (white) glue

polystyrene star

gold glitter paint

scissors

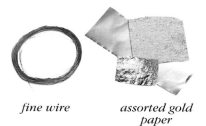

fine wire

assorted gold paper

1 Tear the various gold papers into odd shapes of slightly different sizes.

2 Dilute the PVA (white) glue with a little water. Paint it on to the back of a piece of gold paper and stick on to the polystyrene star. Paint more glue over the piece to secure it. Work all over the front of the star, using different papers to vary the texture and colour.

3 Make a loop of wire and stick the ends into the back of the star for hanging. Secure with masking tape. Cover the back with gold paper in the same way as the front.

4 Leave to dry, then cover with a coat of gold glitter paint.

Velvet Stocking

This rather grown-up stocking is so grand that it's just asking to be filled with exquisite treats and presents. Make it in rich, dark colours for a really Christmassy look.

YOU WILL NEED
paper for templates
dress-weight velvet in three
    toning colours
scissors
pins
tailor's chalk
sewing machine
matching thread
decorative braid
sequin ribbon
gold satin fabric
sewing needle
gold buttons

gold satin fabric

dress-weight velvet

scissors

decorative braid

pins and needle

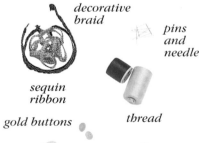

sequin ribbon

gold buttons

thread

tailor's chalk

paper

1 Copy the template for the cuff from the back of the book and increase to the size required. Place the template against a folded edge of the gold satin fabric. Pin and draw around the pattern piece with tailor's chalk. Cut out two cuffs, leaving a narrow seam allowance.

2 As for step 1, make a template for the stocking and divide into three sections. Place the template for each section on a double thickness of each colour velvet. Pin and draw around each piece with tailor's chalk. Cut out, leaving a narrow seam and pin together.

3 Once the three sections of velvet and the gold cuff for each side have been pinned together, machine stitch each seam and tidy any loose ends of thread.

4 On the right side of each piece, pin a strip of decorative braid and a row of sequins. Sew these on invisibly by hand.

5 With right sides together, machine stitch the two sides of the stocking and the cuff together. Turn through, then fold down the gold satin inside to form a deep cuff. Turn in the raw edge of the cuff and stitch down to neaten, catching it to the seams of the velvet stocking.

6 Trim the satin cuff with a few gold buttons and attach a loop of decorative braid for hanging.

Christmas Countdown

Christmas is coming! Excitement builds as the windows of an Advent calendar are opened day by day. Paint the façade of this three-dimensional house in hot, bright colours with lots of gilding.

YOU WILL NEED
tracing paper
pencil
thin white card (cardboard)
craft knife
metal ruler
cutting mat
gouache paints
paintbrush
white cartridge (heavy) paper
watercolour inks
gold (magic) marker pen
glue-stick
white polystyrene-filled
   mounting board
cup sequins

mounting board

watercolour ink

gouache paint

glue-stick

craft knife

metal ruler

cup sequins

pencil

gold (magic) marker pen

white cartridge (heavy) paper

tracing paper

paintbrush

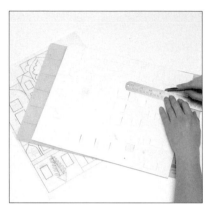

1 Enlarge and trace the template for the front of the Advent calendar and transfer it on to a sheet of white card (cardboard). Cut around three sides of each window with a craft knife.

2 Turn over the sheet and paint the backs of the windows and a little of the area around them with gouache paint, so that they will look neat when the windows are opened.

3 Using the front tracing again, mark the window frames on cartridge (heavy) paper and draw on the inside motifs. Paint with watercolour inks and draw in details with a gold (magic) marker pen. Cut out and attach with a glue-stick.

4 Cut the work into three sections; the first being the main doorway and windows, the second the three middle windows and two towers and the third the top central panel. Cut three pieces of mounting board, making the largest the size of the whole calendar with two more graded steps to go in front.

5 Mount the sections on the boards, gluing the edges, and glue the sections together. Paint the front of the calendar, carefully avoiding getting any paint inside the windows. Add details and number the windows with a gold (magic) marker pen. Don't forget to paint the edges of the mounting boards.

6 Finish the calendar with shiny multi-cup sequins. Using a glue-stick, attach them all around the edges of the Advent calendar.

Needlepoint Pincushion

This pincushion won't take long to stitch and makes a lovely gift for a needlework enthusiast. The starry theme and trimming of glossy cord give it a Christmassy feel, but its subtle shading will make it a joy to use all year round.

YOU WILL NEED
23 cm (9 in) square of white
    needlepoint canvas with 24 holes
    per 5 cm (12 holes per in)
ruler
waterproof (magic) marker pen
masking tape
small lengths of tapestry wool (yarn)
    in 12 shades
scissors
tapestry needle
coordinating furnishing fabric for
    backing
matching thread
needle
polyester wadding (batting)
70 cm (³/₄ yd) decorative cord

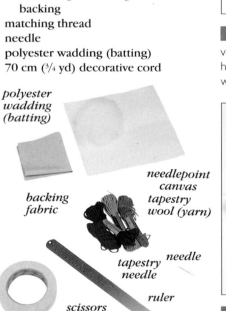

polyester wadding (batting)

backing fabric

needlepoint canvas

tapestry wool (yarn)

tapestry needle

needle

ruler

scissors

masking tape

waterproof (magic) marker pen

decorative cord

thread

1 To prepare the canvas, draw a vertical line down the centre and a horizontal line across the centre with a waterproof (magic) marker pen.

4 Cut a square of backing fabric and pin it to the canvas right sides together. Machine or hand stitch around the edges, leaving a gap on one side. Trim the seams and corners and turn to the right side. Stuff with polyester wadding (batting) to make a nice plump shape.

2 Bind the edges of the canvas with masking tape to prevent the yarn from catching as you work. Select three colours for each corner star.

5 Beginning near the opening, hand stitch the cord around the edges of the cushion. Make a knot in the cord as you reach each corner. Push both ends of the cord into the opening and sew it up neatly, securing the cord as you stitch.

3 Work the design from the chart at the back of the book in tent stitch, beginning in the centre and counting each square as one intersection of canvas threads. Complete all four squares. Remove the masking tape. Press with a steam iron, pulling the canvas gently back into a square. Dry quickly so that the canvas does not distort.

CRAFT TIP

This pincushion is ideal for using up small quantities of tapestry wool (yarn) left over from other projects, but if you do use scraps make sure you will have enough to complete the design.

Yuletide Pot-pourri

Scour ethnic food shops for large bags of bay leaves, cardamom and other exotic ingredients for pot-pourri. Try to include dried flowers (I used hibiscus flowers) for colour and texture.

YOU WILL NEED
oranges
paring knife
large bowl
selection of dried herbs, flowers
    and barks
orris root powder
essential oils
decorative box
cellophane (plastic wrap)
ribbon

large bowl

*cellophane
(plastic wrap)*

*orris root
powder*

essential oils

ribbon

oranges

*paring
knife*

*decorative
box*

*dried herbs,
flowers and barks*

I Pare the rind from several oranges, keeping the strips as long as possible. Dry them in the lowest shelf of a very low oven and store in a dry place until you are ready to use them. Slices of orange can be dried in the same way and are very decorative in pot-pourri.

2 Mix all the ingredients for the pot-pourri in a large bowl. Do not be tempted to use too many different ingredients or the result will be an untidy-looking mixture.

3 Add the orris root powder, which is used as a fixative for the fragrance, sparingly at first: you do not want to see any residue in the finished mixture. Toss the mixture. Sprinkle with your chosen essential oils.

4 Line a decorative box with a large piece of cellophane (plastic wrap) and fill generously with the pot-pourri. Gather up the edges and secure with a ribbon.

Fun Wreath

Although every house deserves an elegant fresh Christmas wreath on the front door, all the family can have plenty of fun making this rather alternative wreath. Think of it as a seasonal joke and load it with all the ephemera of Christmas past and present.

YOU WILL NEED
newspaper
adhesive tape
string
scissors
gold spray paint
hot glue gun
assortment of novelties, candies and
    decorations

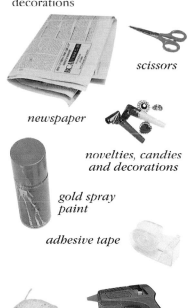

newspaper

scissors

novelties, candies and decorations

gold spray paint

adhesive tape

hot glue gun

string

1 Join two sheets of newspaper together down their short sides with adhesive tape. Scrunch up the paper along its length, squeezing it together while gently twisting it to make a paper rope. When it is quite tightly twisted join the ends with tape to make a ring.

2 Make a second ring in the same way, cutting it a little shorter so that it will fit inside the first ring. Bind the two rings together with string.

3 Spray the ring on both sides with gold paint and leave to dry.

4 Using a hot glue gun, cover the ring completely with an assortment of Christmas ephemera, such as old decorations, cracker novelties, candies, decorated pine cones, and bows from gift wrappings.

Fragrant Herb Pillow

This lovely scented sachet looks as if it has been thickly encrusted with gold. It's made using a cutwork technique in which the different fabrics are revealed as if by magic. It's enjoyable to make and a wonderful gift to receive. Choose fabrics of similar weights but different textures and shades of gold, such as taffeta and lamé.

YOU WILL NEED
four 17 cm (6½ in) squares of
    different gold fabrics
pins
matching thread
sewing machine
sharp-pointed scissors
two 25 cm (10 in) squares of gold
    fabric chosen from the selection
    above
gold braid
needle
fragrant herbs or pot-pourri to fill

gold braid

needle

fragrant herbs
and pot-pourri   pins

thread

sharp-pointed
scissors

selection of
gold fabrics

1 Pin the four 17 cm (6½ in) squares of different gold fabric together, all with right sides facing up.

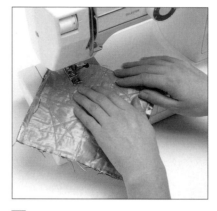

2 Sewing through all four layers, machine stitch across the middle of the square in both directions, then stitch a simple star motif in each quarter. Don't worry if the four stars don't match each other exactly: you are aiming for a freehand effect.

3 With the point of the scissors, pierce the top layer of fabric, then cut out a section of a star. Work around each star, cutting through different areas and layers to reveal the one below until you are pleased with the effect.

4 Pin the appliqué square in the centre of the right side of one of the large squares and machine stitch all around the edge. Hand-stitch a length of gold braid over the seam to hide the raw edges.

5 Pin the other gold square to the front of the cushion, right sides together, and machine around the edge with a 1 cm (½ in) seam allowance, leaving an opening down one side.

CRAFT TIP

It is essential to use really sharp, pointed small scissors for this type of appliqué as you will be cutting away through small areas, some of which may be quite delicate and difficult to manoeuvre around.

6 Turn the work right side out, fill loosely with fragrant herbs or pot-pourri and slip-stitch the opening.

Painted Candles

Plain coloured candles can easily be dressed up for Christmas with gold paint. Use them yourself, but don't forget that they make excellent gifts too. Present them as a set with a coordinating, handmade wrapper.

YOU WILL NEED
coloured candles
gold paint
paintbrush
ribbon
tube of fabric glitter paint
gold gift-wrap
pencil
scissors
cartridge (heavy) paper
watercolour inks

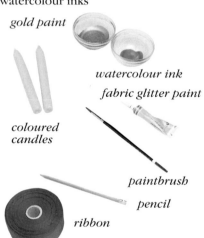

gold paint

watercolour ink

fabric glitter paint

coloured candles

paintbrush

pencil

ribbon

cartridge (heavy) paper

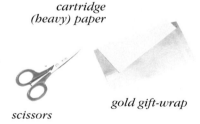

scissors

gold gift-wrap

1 Paint the candles with spots or stripes, building up the colour in several layers if the candles resist the paint. Allow to dry between coats.

2 Apply gold dots on the ribbon with fabric glitter paint. The glitter effect will begin to show only as the paint dries.

3 Fold a strip of gold gift-wrap over several times. Mark a semi-circle at the top and bottom and cut it out. Unfold the paper to reveal a scalloped edge.

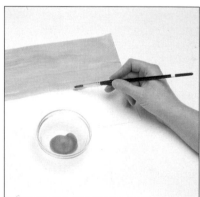

4 Paint a sheet of cartridge (heavy) paper in watercolour ink to coordinate with the candles. Allow to dry then tear into strips. Wrap a set of candles in the scalloped gold paper, then a strip of the painted paper, finishing off with a bow of glitter ribbon.

Painted Card Holders

With your mantelpieces and shelves filled with beautiful decorations, you need to find an attractive and original way to display your Christmas cards. With our painted clothes pegs (pins) and colourful "clothesline", you can hang them all the way up the stairs.

YOU WILL NEED
wooden clothes pegs (pins)
gouache paints
jam jar
paintbrush
thick cotton twine
scissors

gouache paints

scissors

jam jar

paintbrush

thick cotton twine

wooden clothes pegs (pins)

1 Separate the halves of each clothes peg (pin) by removing the spring.

2 Paint the pegs (pins) with gouache paint in an assortment of bright colours. Allow to dry then reassemble.

3 Paint the cotton twine in a bright colour. Allow to dry.

CRAFT TIP

Attach the pegs (pins) to the twine at regular intervals or according to the sizes of cards you are hanging. Leave a good length at each end of the twine for tying.

Front Door Wreath

Take a break from traditional red berries and ribbons with this fresh-looking arrangement. The vibrant orange kumquats are perfectly set off by the cool blue spruce.

YOU WILL NEED
fresh greenery: sprays of bay leaves
    and blue spruce
secateurs (pruning shears)
florist's wire
kumquats
green chillies
pine cones
ready-made willow wreath
wire-edged ribbon
pins
scissors

pine cone

kumquats

green chillies

scissors

secateurs (pruning shears)

pins

fresh greenery

wire-edged ribbon

willow wreath

florist's wire

1 Trim the greenery into sprigs suitable for the size of the wreath, wiring pieces together here and there to fill them out.

2 Twist a piece of wire around each stem, leaving a length to insert into the willow wreath.

3 Wire the kumquats and chillies by sticking a piece of wire through the base then bending the ends down and twisting them together. Wind a piece of wire around the base of each pine cone.

4 Attach the greenery, fruits and cones to the wreath, twisting the ends of the wires to secure them.

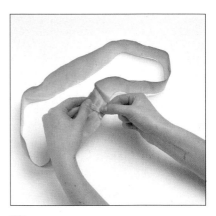

5 Reserving a short length of ribbon for the centre of the bow, join the ends together with a pin.

6 Fold the ribbon over on itself to make four loops.

7 Pinch the centre of the loops together and secure with a wire. Cover this with the remaining piece of ribbon and wire the bow to the wreath.

Picture Bulletin board

Show off your prettiest Christmas cards on this bright and cheerful bulletin board. After the cards have come down it will be equally useful for the rest of the year.

YOU WILL NEED
large picture frame
gold spray paint
piece of soft board to fit snugly
    inside the frame
hessian (burlap) to cover the soft
    board with a 2.5 cm (1in)
    overhang
staple gun
ribbons in various widths and
    colours
drawing pins (thumb tacks)

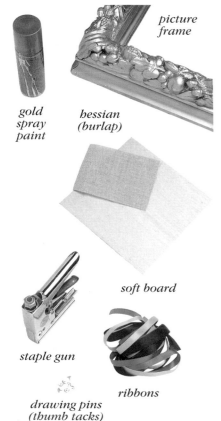

gold spray paint

picture frame

hessian (burlap)

soft board

staple gun

ribbons

drawing pins (thumb tacks)

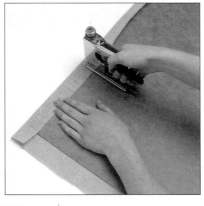

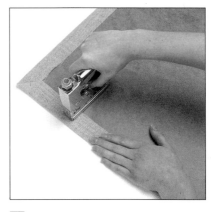

1 Clean and repair your frame if it is an old one. Spray with gold paint and allow it to dry.

2 Cover the soft board with the hessian (burlap), securing the edges at the back with a staple gun. Make sure the fabric is evenly stretched, securing it at points opposite one another.

3 Fold the corners neatly and secure the fabric all around the edge of the board.

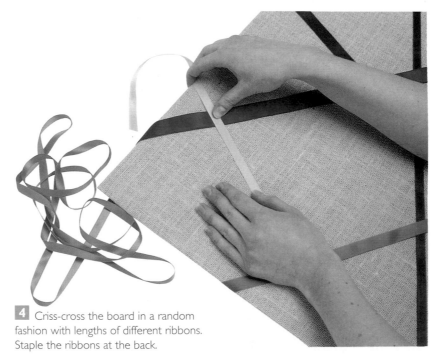

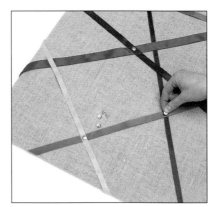

4 Criss-cross the board in a random fashion with lengths of different ribbons. Staple the ribbons at the back.

5 Secure the ribbons with drawing pins (thumb tacks) at each point where they cross. Place the board inside the frame.

Collage Gift-wrap

Look along the racks on the newspaper stand for interesting foreign scripts to incorporate in this fascinating gift-wrap. The newspaper is painted with translucent watercolour inks so that the print shows through.

YOU WILL NEED
foreign language newspaper
watercolour inks
paintbrush
white cartridge (heavy) paper
coloured card (cardboard)
stencil card (cardboard)
craft knife
gold and black stencil paint
cellulose kitchen sponge
scissors
corrugated cardboard
plain gold gift-wrap
glue-stick

watercolour ink

stamp

stencil paint

stencil card and white card (cardboard)

coloured card (cardboard)

stencil brush

foreign language newspaper

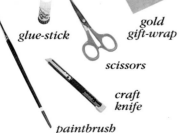

glue-stick

gold gift-wrap

scissors

craft knife

paintbrush

1 Paint sections of the newspaper in bright watercolour inks.

2 Transfer the Christmas tree template at the back of the book to a piece of stencil card (cardboard) and cut out. Paint plain white cartridge (heavy) paper in different coloured inks or use coloured card (cardboard). Stencil the paper in black and gold.

3 Cut a triangular Christmas tree shape out of kitchen sponge and stick it to a piece of corrugated cardboard. Stamp some of the coloured newsprint with gold trees.

4 Tear strips, rectangles and simple tree shapes from the coloured newsprint. Tear around the stamped and stencilled motifs, and cut some out with scissors to give a different texture.

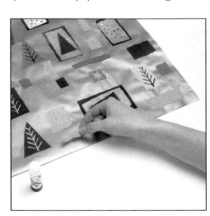

5 Arrange the motifs on the gold gift-wrap and attach them down using a glue-stick.

Christmas Tree Gift Tags

As with the gift-wrap on the previous pages, spend some time making yourself a selection of stamped, stencilled and painted motifs before you begin to assemble the gift tags.

YOU WILL NEED
craft knife
metal ruler
cutting mat
thin card (cardboard) in
    various colours
tracing paper
pencil
paper for templates
cellulose kitchen sponge
scissors
corrugated cardboard
glue-stick
stencil paint in gold and black
stencil card (cardboard)
white cartridge (heavy) paper
paintbrush
watercolour inks
white oil crayon
brown parcel wrap (packaging
    paper)
hole punch
fine gold cord

stencil paint

watercolour ink

scissors

paper

thin card (cardboard)

fine gold cord

tracing paper

glue-stick

stencil card (cardboard)

brown parcel wrap (packaging paper)

white cartridge (heavy) paper

metal ruler

hole punch

craft knife

paintbrush

white oil crayon

1 Using a craft knife and a metal ruler, cut out tags from thin card (cardboard) in various colours.

2 Trace the Christmas tree motif from the back of the book and make a paper template. Draw around this on a rectangle of kitchen sponge and cut out carefully with scissors, so that you have a positive and negative image to use as stamps. Mount each stamp on a piece of cardboard with a glue-stick. Stamp both motifs in gold on to a selection of papers in different textures and colours (use tracing paper as well).

3 Trace the Christmas tree branch pattern and transfer it to a piece of stencil card. Cut out using a craft knife and stencil in black and gold on to a selection of papers and on some of the stamped motifs.

4 Paint plain white cartridge (heavy) paper with watercolour ink in bright colours and cut out a simple star motif.

80

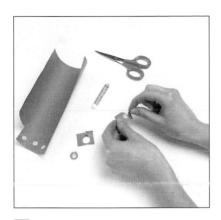

5 Use a white oil crayon to scribble spots on brown parcel wrap (packaging paper) for snowflakes. Tear them out individually leaving a border of brown paper around each one.

6 Assemble the tags. Cut or tear out a selection of motifs and arrange them on the cards. Attach with the glue-stick. Punch a hole in the top and thread each with a loop of fine gold cord.

Crayon Gift-wrap

See how easy it can be to transform humble brown parcel wrap (packaging paper) into stylish and original gift-wraps. Both suggestions are quick to do but allow at least 24 hours for the oil pastels to dry before using the paper.

YOU WILL NEED
brown parcel wrap (packaging paper)
masking tape
gold paint
old plate
sponge roller
gold oil crayon
oil pastel crayons in black, white and colours

brown parcel wrap (packaging paper)

masking tape

gold paint

oil pastel crayons

gold oil crayon

sponge roller

old plate

1 Secure the brown parcel wrap (packaging paper) with masking tape. Spread gold paint on an old plate. Using a sponge roller, apply the paint in wide gold lines up the sheet. Leave to dry.

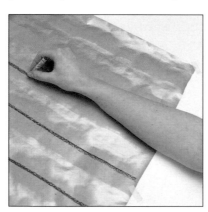

2 Add coloured or just black and white stripes to the gold. Leave the paper to dry thoroughly before using.

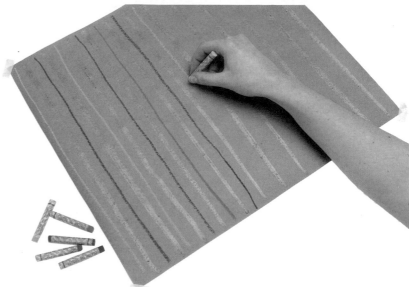

3 For an alternative look, draw vertical stripes down a piece of brown parcel wrap (packaging paper) with a chunky gold oil crayon. Experiment with different groupings and spacings for the stripes. Make several sheets to work on further.

Tin Gift Box

Embossed aluminium foil combines festive glitter with the gentle naïve appeal of tinware, and it's a perfect match for the simplicity of this Shaker box. The embossing is easy to do – simple designs really are the most successful.

YOU WILL NEED
tracing paper
heavy-gauge aluminium foil
masking tape
dried-out ballpoint pen
scissors
gift box
glue-stick

scissors

glue-stick *heavy gauge aluminium foil*

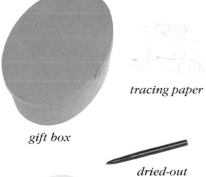

tracing paper

gift box

dried-out ballpoint pen

masking tape

1 Trace the reindeer and stars motifs from the back of the book. Attach the tracings to the foil with masking tape and draw over the outlines with a dried-out ballpoint pen.

2 Remove the tracing paper and go over the embossing again if necessary. Cut out the motifs with scissors, leaving a narrow border of about 2 mm (¹/₁₆ in) around the edge – don't cut into the embossing.

3 Add more embossed details to the motifs if you wish.

4 Turn the motifs over and arrange them on the box lid and sides. Attach them using a glue-stick applied liberally.

Place Marker Gift Bags

With these pretty copper foil tags you can plan your seating arrangement by numbers. Fill the little bags with appropriate small gifts for your dinner-party guests.

CRAFT TIP
When you're embossing metallic foil, remember that you'll be working from the back of the finished design, so always draw the motif on to the foil in reverse.

YOU WILL NEED
metallic crepe paper in bronze
craft knife
metal ruler
double-sided adhesive
    (cellophane) tape
tracing paper
heavy-gauge copper foil
dried-out ballpoint pen
scissors
hole punch
fine gold cord
gifts to go in the bags
ribbon

dried-out ballpoint pen

ribbon

metallic crepe paper in bronze

double-sided adhesive (cellophane) tape

masking tape

craft knife

scissors

fine gold cord

tracing paper

metal ruler

hole punch

heavy-gauge copper foil

1 Cut a rectangle of the crepe paper 45 × 42 cm (18 × 16½ in).

2 Fold over 15 cm (6 in) along one of the long sides, for the top, and 1.5 cm (⅝ in) along the other for the bottom of the bag.

3 Use double-sided adhesive (cellophane) tape to stick together the sides of the bag and then the bottom edge of the bag.

4 Trace the numeral needed for each place setting, then transfer the design in reverse to the copper foil, embossing it with a dried-out ballpoint pen.

5 Cut out the numeral with scissors. Punch a hole in the top and thread with fine gold cord.

6 Fill the bag with a suitable gift, then close. Tie the ribbon in a bow around the neck of the bag and finally attach the metal tag.

Crepe Paper Carrier Bags

When you have to wrap an awkwardly shaped gift, or a number of small things that go together, a carrier bag is a good solution. With this easy method of bag-making, you just wrap the paper around a book as if you were wrapping a package. Pull out the book and there's your bag. Match the book to the size of your gift.

YOU WILL NEED
crepe paper
book
craft knife
metal ruler
cutting mat
scissors
double-sided adhesive
    (cellophane) tape
hole punch
ribbon
chocolate coin

book

metal ruler

crepe paper

scissors

ribbon

chocolate coin

double-sided adhesive (cellophane) tape

craft knife

ribbon

hole punch

1 Place the book on top of the crepe paper and measure and mark the rectangle you will need to wrap the book with an overlap of 1.5 cm (⅝ in). Trim using a craft knife and metal ruler.

2 Using scissors, score a fold about 4 cm (1½ in) from one long edge and fold it down to form the top of the bag.

3 Fold the paper over the book neatly and secure the sides with double-sided adhesive (cellophane) tape.

4 Fold in the bottom edge as if you were wrapping a package and secure to ensure the bag will take the weight of the gift. Remove the book.

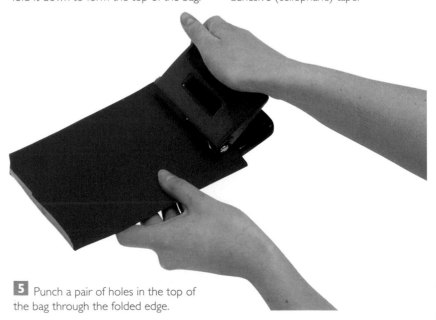

5 Punch a pair of holes in the top of the bag through the folded edge.

6 Thread a length of ribbon through the holes and knot the ends on the inside of the bag.

7 Decorate the bag with a chocolate coin arranged on two short lengths of ribbon to look like a medal.

TEMPLATES

ENLARGING TEMPLATES

If the templates need to be enlarged, and you do not have access to a photocopier, you can use the grid system. Trace the template and draw a grid of evenly-spaced squares over your tracing. To scale up, draw a larger grid on to another piece of paper. Copy the outline on to the second grid by taking each square individually and drawing the relevant part of the outline in the larger square. Finally, draw over the lines to make sure they are continuous.

GILDED CHRISTMAS PLATE

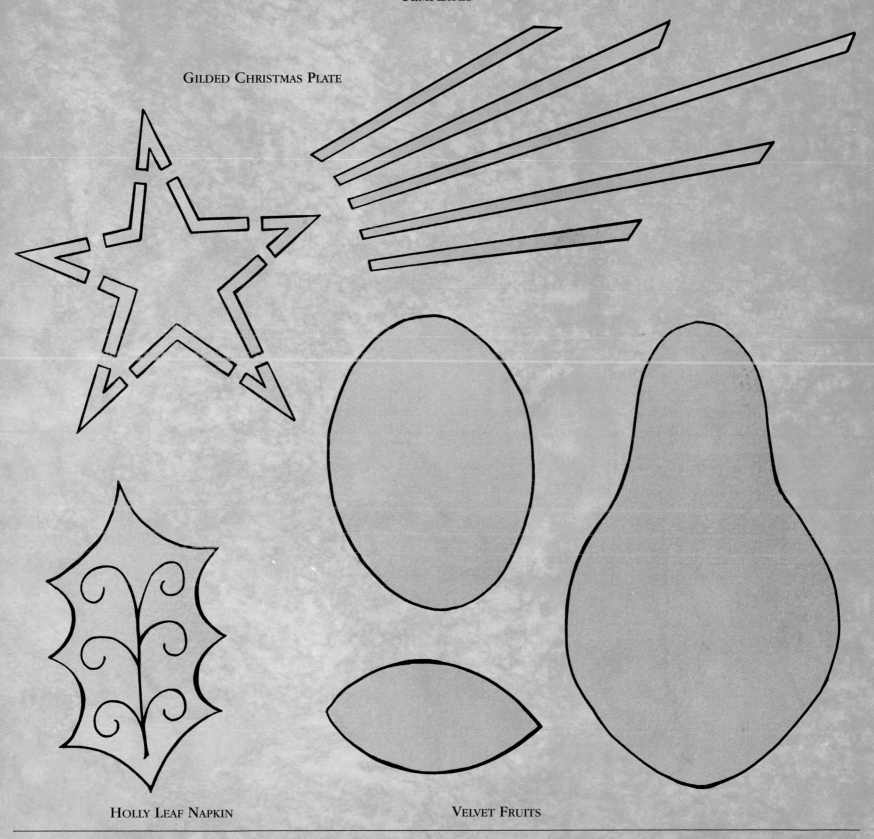

GILDED CHRISTMAS PLATE

HOLLY LEAF NAPKIN

VELVET FRUITS

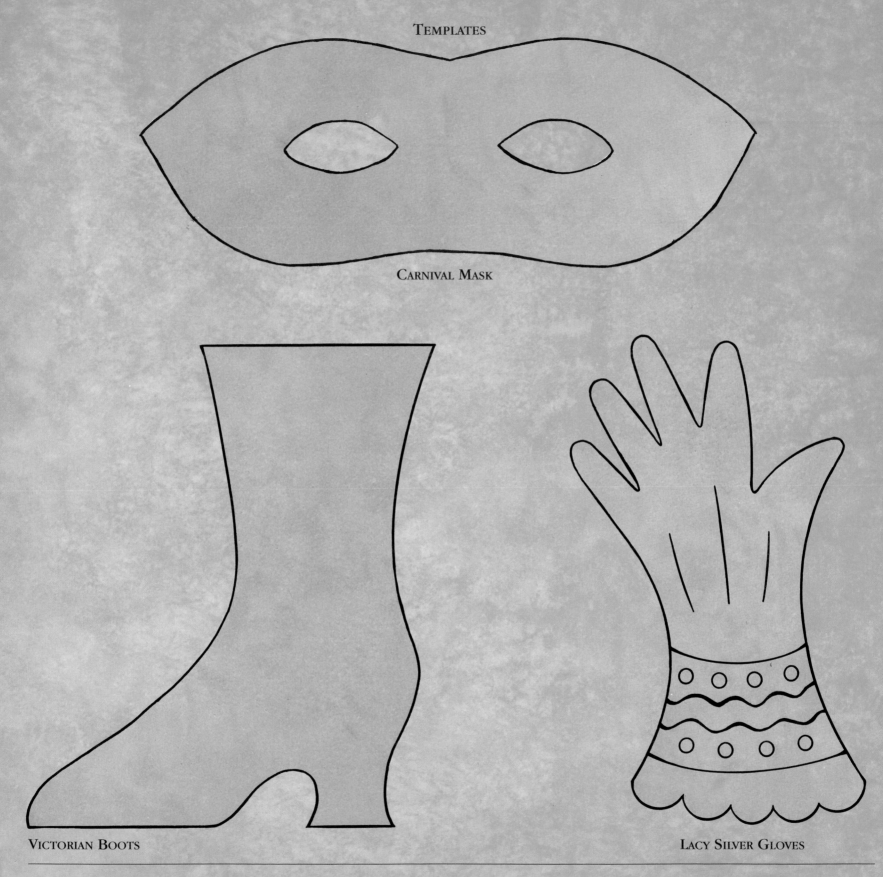

CARNIVAL MASK

VICTORIAN BOOTS

LACY SILVER GLOVES

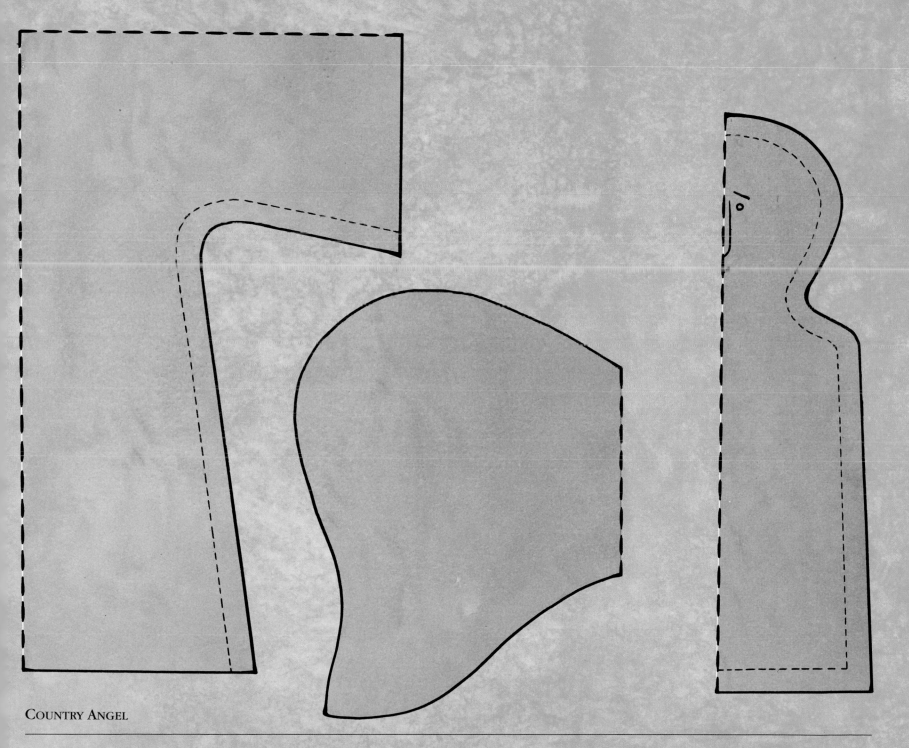

COUNTRY ANGEL

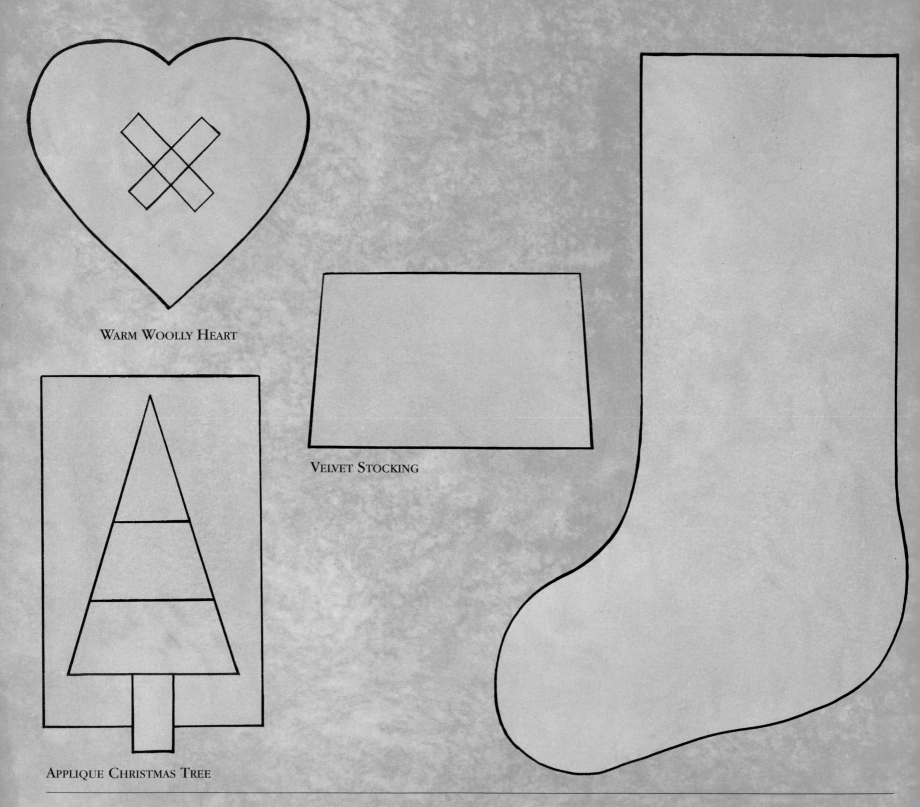

WARM WOOLLY HEART

VELVET STOCKING

APPLIQUE CHRISTMAS TREE

COLLAGE GIFT-WRAP AND
CHRISTMAS TREE GIFT TAGS

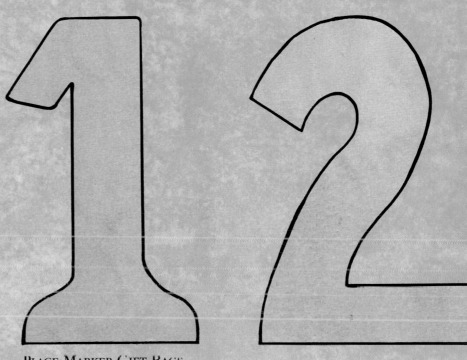

PLACE MARKER GIFT BAGS

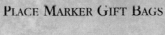

TIN GIFT BOX

INDEX

A

Adhesive tape, 12
Advent calendar, 64
Angel, country, 50
Appliqué Christmas tree, 60

B

Balls, raffia, 52
Beads, 10
Blanket stitch, 15
Boots, Victorian, 41
Braids, 10
Bulletin Board, picture
    frame, 76
Button garland, 49
Buttons, 10
    pearl houses and hearts,
    56

C

Calico, 10
Candle-holders silver crown,
    27
    star, 22
Candle pot, silk-wrapped, 32
Candles: Christmas
    mantelpiece, 34
    painted, 72
Canvas, tapestry, 10
Card holder, painted, 73
Carnival mask, 44
Carrier bags, crepe paper, 87
Checked cotton, 10
Christmas countdown, 64
Christmas crackers, 36
Christmas mantelpiece, 34
Christmas plate, gilded, 20
Christmas tree: appliqué, 60
    white, 30
Christmas tree gift tags, 80
Citrus centrepiece, 38
Collage gift-wrap, 78
Cookies for the tree, 48
Cords, 10
Cotton, checked, 10
Country angel, 50
Crackers, 36
Craft knife, 12
Crayon gift-wrap, 82
Crayons, 8
Crepe paper carrier bags, 86

D

Decorative papers, 8

E

Emulsion paint, 8
Equipment, 12
Exotic ornaments, 47

F

Fabrics, 10
Festive wine glasses, 19
Flowerpot, sparkling, 26
Foam rollers, 12
Foils, metal, 8
Fragrant herb pillow, 70
French knots, 15
Front door wreath, 74
Fruits, velvet, 28
Fun wreath, 69

G

Gift bags, 84
Gift box, tin, 83
Gift tags, Christmas tree, 80
    stamps, 17
Gift-wrap: collage, 78
    crayon, 82
Gilded Christmas plate, 20
Gilded glass spheres, 18
Gilded rosettes, 46
Gingerbread cookies, 48
Glass spheres, gilded, 18
Glitter, 8
Glitter keys, 42
Gloves, lacy silver, 45
Glue, 12
Gold crown tablecloth, 24

H

Heavenly gold star, 61
Herb pillow, 70
Hessian (burlap), 10
Hole punch, 12
Holly leaf napkin, 25
Hot glue gun, 12

K

Keys: glitter, 42
    ornamental, 43

L

Lacy silver gloves, 45

Lamé, 10
Lemons and limes: citrus
    centrepiece, 38
Lino-cutting tool, 8

M

Mask, carnival, 44
Materials, 8
Metal foils, 8
    working with, 17
Metal ruler, 12

N

Napkin, holly leaf, 25
Napkin rings, willow twig, 33
Needlepoint pincushion, 66
Needlepoint tent stitch, 14

O

Oil-based paints, 8
Oranges: citrus centrepiece,
    38
Organza (organdy), 10
Ornamental keys, 43
Ornaments, exotic, 47

P

Paintbrushes, 12
Painted candles, 72
Painted bulletin board, 76
Paints: glitter, 8
    oil-based, 8
    types of, 8
    white emulsion (latex), 8
Paper: decorative, 8
    types of, 8
Picture frame bulletin board,
    73
Pincushion, needlepoint, 66
Pins and needles, 12
Place marker gift bags, 84
Plastic adhesive, 12
Polyester wadding (batting),
    10
Polystyrene shapes (forms), 8
Pot-pourri, Yuletide, 68
Purses, silk, 40

R

Raffia, 10
Raffia balls, 52
Ribbons, 10

Rollers, foam, 12
Rosettes, gilded, 46
Ruler, metal, 12

S

Santa's toy sack, 58
Saucers and jars, 12
Scissors, 12
Secateurs (pruning shears),
    12
Sequins, 10
Silk purses, 40
Silk-wrapped candle pot, 32
Silks, 10
Silver crown candle-holder,
    27
Socks, knitted, 54
Sparkling flowerpot, 26
Stamping, 17
Stapler, 12
Star: candle-holder, 22
    heavenly god, 61
Stem stitch, 14
Stencil card, 12
Stencilling, 16
Stitches: blanket stitch, 15
    French knots, 15
    needlepoint tent stitch, 14
    stem stitch, 14
Stocking, velvet, 62
String, 10

T

Tablecloth, gold crown, 24
Taffeta, 10
Tape, adhesive, 12
Tapestry canvas, 10
Templates, 88-95
    making, 16
Threads, 10
Tin gift box, 83
Toy sack, 58
Tree decorations
    button garland, 49
    cookies, 48
    country angel, 50
    gilded rosettes, 46
    glitter keys, 42
    ornamental keys, 43
    pearl houses and hearts,
    56
    raffia balls, 52

silk purses, 40
tiny knitted socks, 54
twiggy stars, 53
Victorian boots, 41
warm woolly heart, 57
Trims, 10
Twiggy stars, 53

V

Velvet, 10
Velvet fruits, 28
Velvet stocking, 62
Victorian boots, 41

W

Wadding (batting), polyester,
    10
Warm woolly heart, 57
White Christmas tree, 30
Willow twigs, 8
    napkin rings, 33
    twiggy stars, 53
Wine glasses, festive, 19
Wool, 10
Wreaths
    front door, 74
    fun, 69

Y

Yuletide pot-pourri, 68

ACKNOWLEDGEMENTS

The author would like to
thank Bridget Honour for the
Stencilled Tablecloth and
Painted Plate and Judy Dann
for the Velvet Fruits. Thanks
also to Panduro Hobby,
Transport Avenue, Brentford,
Middlesex, TW8 8BR. Tel:
01392 4227788 for supplying
craft equipment.